THE DOCTORS IN THE TEMPLE *were astounded at Jesus' intelligence and His questions. Afterwards He went home with Mary and Joseph to Nazareth where He "grew in wisdom, in stature, and favor with God and men"* (Luke 2:52)

Growing in Grace

Growing in Grace

by Alfred McBride, O.Praem.

GOOD WILL PUBLISHERS, INC.
Gastonia, North Carolina

Library of Congress Catalog Number: 72-92780

NIHIL OBSTAT
    Bernard L. Rosswog, O.S.B., S.T.D.
    Censor Librorum

IMPRIMATUR
    ✠ Edmund F. McCaffrey, O.S.B., Ph.D., D.D.
    Abbot-Ordinary, Diocese of Belmont Abbey Nullius

ACKNOWLEDGMENTS

    Editorial Director, **John P. Bradley**

    Full color illustrations are reproductions of original paintings by
    George Malick

    Line drawings are by Georgette Delattre.

Printed in the United States of America

Contents

6   CONTENTS

8   **CONTENTS**

Introduction

ALL THE GREAT RELIGIONS of the world begin with stories. The reason is that a story is one of the best ways of showing how God is present to every part of life. Originally, the Bible was not a written word, but a spoken word. It was Holy Word before it was Holy Writ. The poets, bards, and minstrels of Israel spoke and sang these ancient stories from generation to generation.

THE STORY OF MAN'S LIFE WITH GOD

Each evening by the firelight the tales of the heroes, saints, kings, prophets, patriarchs, and warriors were told and retold. With each passing age, the narratives grew richer as new sagas of man's life with God unfolded. Lest in some way the stories might be lost they were reverently written down. Thus they were "canonized" as the Holy Word, that is, they *really* reflected God's intimate love affair with man.

That is why the Bible is best understood when read aloud. The text is rich enough to be tasted, and textured enough to be felt. In the old synagogues of Eastern Europe they used to celebrate the "ceremony of God's sweetness." Very young children were brought to the synagogue for their first introduction to the Bible. A great old book was brought out and opened. Some honey was placed on the page and the child was invited to taste of the sweetness. In this way his first experience of God's word was pleasant.

THE INSPIRATION OF GREAT MEN AND WOMEN

The Bible inspires men to live in honest relationship with God and fellow man. Countless great men and women have cited the

Bible as their greatest source of light and hope. It is not only the book of saints; it is also the book that helps make saints.

Remember Thomas More, the man for all seasons? "I am the king's true subject and pray for him and all the realm. I do none harm. I say none harm. And if this be not enough to keep a man alive, in good faith, I long not to live." Thomas More knew the power of Scripture.

Remember Damien who brought the Holy Word to the lepers at Molokai? He felt the spirit of the Bible.

"Sooner or later you will catch the disease yourself."

"Yes, I know, but I must go."

"Once you go, you may never be allowed to return."

"I must go to Molokai."

GETTING TO KNOW THE MEANING OF THE BIBLE

Often we are afraid of something simply because we don't understand it. Too many people are afraid of really trying to get to know the meaning of the Bible because they fear they just won't understand it. I realize that parts of it are strange. However, the purpose of this book is to help you to see that it's really not so strange when you understand it better. In the Bible we find quarreling brothers, jealous kings, noble patriotism, witches, heroic women, youthful prophets, and peaceful men of wisdom. It knows all about wars, dances, revolutions, love, pioneering, and exile. Every major human feeling, failing, and triumph are included in its pages.

NO SUBSTITUTE FOR THE BIBLE ITSELF

My method has not been to concentrate on the story since you can find that for yourself in the Bible. I have tried to provide the message of each story and the necessary details of history and fashions so that the meaning will be clear to you. This is a guide-book, and therefore not a substitute for the real thing.

The pictures have been carefully selected to give you a visual peg for the material. None of this is meant to curb your own way of picturing the great events in the drama of man's adventures with God.

In almost every instance I have attempted to find some modern image or example that matches up with the biblical tales. It is my hope that you will go on to make your own comparisons and applications to your personal life. Never forget, however, that the Holy Word itself has the most importance. Like a good rain on fertile earth, it always works its own magic:

> For as the rain and the snow
>   come down from heaven,
> and return not there, but water the earth,
>   making it bring forth and sprout,
>   giving seed to the sower and
>   bread to the eater,
> so shall my Word be that goes forth from my mouth;
> it shall not return to me empty [Isaiah 55:10–11].

This guidebook, then, is intended to lead you to that nourishment that God's Holy Word alone can give you—the divine nourishment through which you will "grow in grace." And this means that as you grow physically in stature, you will also grow "in wisdom and in favor with God and men" (Luke 2:52).

CREATION
Man Is the Image of God

The Bible's description of creation gives us an earth's eye-view of the ordered universe (the cosmos). In the geography of the times, the earth was considered to be flat. It rested on an ocean of water. Seas and rivers were places where this ocean pierced through the earth's surface. The sky was like an astrodome neatly fitted to the edges of the earth. Its purpose was to keep out the waters on the upper level. The sun, moon, and stars were like electric lights screwed into the sky-ceiling which the Bible calls the firmament. In the firmament, also, were trapdoors which God occasionally opened to let in some rain.

The people of these ancient times believed that one could fall off the edge of the earth into the great ocean if he walked far enough in a set direction.

THE SPIRIT OF GOD DREW ORDER FROM DISORDER

Not having our scientific knowledge, the people of ancient times naturally saw the world this way because that is how it presented itself to them. To their minds, the basic element was the ocean, a surrounding and terrifying chaos (trackless waste and emptiness).

It was out of this chaos that God drew the cosmos. "The earth was without form and void, and darkness was upon the face of the deep [chaos]." Over this formless chaos roamed the creative breath of God, called His Spirit. "And the Spirit of God was moving over the face of the waters" (Genesis 1:2).

Hence, the breath which is God hovered over the waters of chaos and drew forth the cosmos. Here we have a theme which will be carried out many times in the Bible — bringing Noah's family out of the chaos of the deluge, saving Lot's family from the chaos of Sodom and Gomorrah as the salt sea surrounded it, rescuing Israel from the chaotic waters of the Red Sea, and drawing Jesus forth from the waters of the Jordan to inaugurate a new creation.

DANIEL'S VISION

Some observers have been inclined to tie up the creation story here with the vision of Daniel (see page 165). The Bible tells us that Daniel had a vision of a black lake out of which came four monsters. The four winds, or God's breath, hovered over the waters before the emergence of the monsters (Daniel 7).

What Daniel seems to be saying is that the first creation resulted in the appearance of men who refused to image God, and so became the tyrants who ruled the earth for their own selfish purposes. But, even more important is that the word for "create" in the book of Daniel implies fatherhood. The creator is a father who sires a son from whom he wishes a son's response. Creation, then, has the quality of sonship about it. This is best expressed in the obedience and love of mankind to whom is entrusted the lordship of the earth. Daniel's vision ends with the preview of a new mankind who will be faithful and responsive.

MANY ANCIENT PEOPLES HAD CREATION STORIES

Ever since the explosion of archeological studies there has been a tendency to see, in the literature of other cultures, comparisons

"IN THE BEGINNING God created the heavens and the earth. The earth was without form and void, and darkness was upon the face of the deep; and the Spirit of God was moving over the face of the waters" (Genesis 1:1–2)

to the stories found in the Bible. Archeologists have found creation stories among the Babylonians that show similarities to the biblical accounts. The Babylonian creation myth, "Enuma Elish," speaks of a titanic battle between the goddess Tiamat and Marduk. *Tiamat* means "chaos." She is slain by Marduk.

Then he, together with another character named Bel, carve up her carcass to make the earth. For biblical studies, the point to be made here is that creation is a process whereby the cosmos is produced out of the chaos. Just doing a little word study enforces the point. Tiamat comes from the word *tehom* meaning chaos. In turn, *tehom* is a sister word to *tohu* which is part of the biblical word for chaos.

The beauty of comparing the biblical tale to the Babylonian one is seen in the restraint and dignity of the biblical text. Gone is the grisly carving scene. The violence of the Babylonian myth gives way to the serene poetry of the biblical text.

THE HEBREWS SAW CREATION AS AN ONGOING PROCESS

Generally, the question of evolution arises whenever the creation story comes up. What is this matter of the six days? Can we reconcile the theory of evolution with the biblical narrative? As to the six days, we have the matter of the rabbinic teaching about the sabbath. Hebrew religion stressed that the seventh day should be a time of reflecting on the meaning of God and human existence. To reinforce this act of piety, they described God as a Hebrew laborer who rests on the seventh day. The faithful Israelite could do no better than imitate the Lord in this regard.

Concerning the matter of evolution, the verb forms used in the creation story are dynamic, not static. In Hebrew, the atmosphere of creation is one of process, not of a finished task. It is not as though creation happened and then is all over with. Rather, creation is something that begins and continues. The process of removing the chaos and bringing about order is a continuous task.

THE BREATH WHICH IS GOD *hovered over the waters of chaos and drew forth the cosmos*

God begins the work of creation and fathers forth a world which is to be like a son to Him. But ultimately, He brings forth man and woman who shall be the lords of the world and continue His work. Certainly, the Hebrew authors were not thinking of the theory of evolution. It was not a problem for them.

These authors used the poetry of the seven days to defend the sabbath rest. They used dynamic verb forms to show that creation was a process of bringing order out of chaos, and that this was a work common to mankind as imaging the Lord. They didn't do this as a concession to Darwin. It was simply their normal way of understanding the creation event.

GOD CREATED MAN IN HIS OWN IMAGE

More than likely the creation story as we now have it was written by Israelite clergymen. So much of the language used reminds us of the liturgy which is the central concern of priests. Creation is described in terms of the temple. The word for firmament is borrowed from the word used for the roof of the Jerusalem temple. The words for the sun and stars were taken from the names used for lighting equipment in the temple. God's blessing of creation ("He saw that it was good") is similar to the clerical blessings normally given in the temple. In other words, the temple was the symbol of the really great temple of creation established by God.

Both prophets and priests throughout Israelite history strove to keep the people from idolatry. They insisted that no carved item could be an image of God. They were never totally successful. Images of cherubim were allowed to hold up the ark of the covenant. The priestly theologians eventually arrived at the insight that the real image of God is man. No image could be better. "So God created man in His own image" (Genesis 1:27).

WHAT IT MEANS TO BE THE IMAGE OF GOD

To be the image of God meant two things. First, man was expected to continue the work of creation. He was to bring life to the earth, develop the potentiality of the land, and do both of these things for the sake of human concern. Second, in so acting, man manifested the creative wisdom of God and, therefore, the presence of God Himself. God's presence breaks through in the lives of men who imitate His creative thrust and celebrate His wisdom in the heart of the earth. Daniel's dream showed that men became tyrants, and did not manage the earth out of love for men. Hence a new man had to come.

This new man was Jesus, the most perfect image of God this earth has known. "He is the image of the invisible God, the firstborn of all creation" (Colossians 1:15). Today's Christians should remember their call to image God. They should rejoice that this is made more possible now because Christ has shown us the way and given us the power.

MAN IS A REBEL
The Story of Adam and Eve

Probably no Old Testament story has been retold more often than the fascinating story of Adam and Eve. It has been approached in many different ways. Moralists examine it for information on original sin. Biblical theologians wrestle with the comparisons between the old Adam and Christ, the new Adam. Archeologists, historians, and poets are also interested in this story from their own special viewpoints.

ORIGINAL SIN: THE HUMAN CONDITION

We can approach the story of Adam and Eve profitably by looking at some of the interests mentioned above. Certainly, the concern of the moralists is important in the Adam and Eve story, for from it they have derived the doctrine of original sin. It is true that the term "original sin" does not appear in the Bible. It seems to have been formulated first by Saint Augustine in the fourth century. There have been many fuzzy thoughts on the matter of original sin, thoughts which are inaccurate, and are supported neither by the Bible nor by theologians.

For one thing, original sin is not a stain on the soul; nor do we inherit it biologically from our parents, like red hair or blue eyes. It is no simple matter to say exactly what original sin is. The biblical story describes it as an act of disobedience which caused Adam and Eve to fall from their ideal state of living. Now, given the fact that the last editing of the Adam and Eve story was done after the Exile, about 400 B.C. (*see* page 134), it seems that the narrative is a verdict of Hebrew theologians on the state of mankind. They consider the history of the people of God, from their dimmest origins all the way through to the period after the Exile, and they see the extent of the human predicament.

These theologians notice that the theme of disobedience and falling short of ideals is repeated constantly throughout sacred history. Rarely, if ever, has any man achieved the ideal set for him by God. Hence, they came to see that what happened in Eden also happened in the exodus experience (*see* pages 66–70), the time of the Judges (*see* pages 82–86), the era of the monarchy (*see* pages 87–101; 107–124), and even after the tragedy of the Exile. The constant statement of history is that mankind is a rebel. The story of the fall of man from the garden of happiness is a miniature recital of the history of mankind. It seems to say that mankind never achieves the ideal set for it by God. Universally, men rebel against God.

The result is that men are enslaved by the tyrannies of the human condition. They live on the earth as aliens, estranged from God and from their fellowmen. The land, the sea, the animals – all seem to pull away from man and appear hostile to him. Man stands alone in a hostile universe which threatens to snuff him out. This is the result of his rebellion against God and the purpose which God set for man in the world.

Saint Paul sensed the anguish of this human predicament and cried out: "Wretched man that I am! Who will deliver me from

THE ADAM AND EVE STORY *teaches us that mankind never achieves the ideal set for us by God—man rebels against God*

this body of death? [the state of original sin]. Thanks be to God [I will be delivered] through Jesus Christ our Lord" (Romans 7:24).

GARDEN OF EDEN STORY AND BABYLONIAN GARDENS

The archeologists compare the story to cultural themes in Babylonian life. Their conclusion is that the pictorial features of the story of the Garden of Eden are taken from Hebrew memories of their life in Babylon during the Exile. Many of them worked as gardeners and landscapers on the vast estates of their Babylonian masters. Most estates had fruit orchards, and some of the trees were highly cultivated to produce exceptional fruit. These were the masters' favorite trees, and the workers were strictly forbidden to touch such trees or take any of the fruit. If they stole the fruit they would be fired from the estate.

Around these estates were large walls. At the gates it was common to have decorations. Sometimes, carved on these gates were powerful winged creatures brandishing fiery swords. These figures served as symbolic guardians of the masters' lands. It is felt that this situation provided the sacred writer with powerful and memorable material to describe the rebellion of man. Adam and Eve were like Hebrew gardeners on a Babylonian estate. Against strict orders they stole fruit from the favored tree, and so were fired from the garden of happiness. At the gates were the fiery guards forbidding their re-entry into the master's house.

Whether or not this interpretation is true, it does place before us the honest effort of modern scholars to probe the cultural background of the story. It has convincing arguments, but time is yet needed to test the theory. At least, it brings us to reflect that the story was written by men who wanted to present a vivid and relevant account of the fall of man in a way the readers would best understand.

THE STORY OF ADAM AND EVE *relates that because of their disobedience they were banished from the Garden of Eden. Rarely, if ever, has any man achieved the ideal set for him by God*

ALL MEN LINKED TO EACH OTHER

Poets turn to the garden story for a confirmation of their ideas about the solidarity of mankind. This is a difficult idea to grasp. While on the one hand, man stands alone in the world, on the other, he is vitally linked to all other men.

The present political state of our world is one way of understanding the solidarity of mankind. In years past, nations tended to be interested only in themselves; they were fiercely nationalistic and isolationist. But that was in a world in which nations were separated by vast geographical expanses and had few means of communication.

Today, isolationism and nationalism have become dangerous, for the world has become a village in which events at all points of the globe have a vital influence on all the others. War in Palestine causes fear throughout the world. The hitherto unknown country of Vietnam became the center of the United States' national interest. Every statement of world leaders attracts the attention of the whole world.

This situation throughout the world helps us to understand the poets' insight into the solidarity of mankind. They see what Saint Paul meant when he claimed that in Adam all men fell, and in Christ all men can find salvation. "For as by one man's disobedience many were made sinners, so by one man's obedience many will be made righteous" (Romans 5:19).

The story of Adam and Eve will always be a source of interest and fresh speculation. The lines of thought it opens for the inquiring Christian are varied and vast. It is important to separate pure theorizing from genuine teaching and prudent conclusion. In the treasury of Scripture, few statements about the relation of man to God are more powerful. In our time, when such a relation is again being considered with utmost seriousness, the story of the garden of happiness reflects its ancient and ever-new light.

A STORY WITH MANY MEANINGS
Cain and Abel

Anyone who has ever had a brother knows the kind of rivalry that can easily grow between brothers. In the Cain and Abel story, this rivalry is carried to its extreme form in Cain's murderous hatred of Abel that ended in Abel's death. The meaning of this story is far greater than the account of a murder in the distant mists of history. The Israelites saw in the tale three different levels of meaning that concerned: (1) the change from pastoral to city life; (2) the hostility between Israel, the northern kingdom, and Judah the southern kingdom (*see* page 117); (3) freedom of worship granted by the Israelites to the neighboring Kenite tribe. We shall consider each of these in turn.

THE CHANGE FROM PASTORAL TO CITY LIFE

In her earliest days, Israel had been a pastoral community wandering from place to place with her sheep. The Israelites associated their nomadic existence in the desert of Sinai with the intense religious experience of the covenant and the giving of the ten commandments (*see* page 72). Their memory of this life evoked the idealism of the founding fathers and of the unstained purity of real religion.

As they settled into urban life, established a monarchy, and organized their nation, there arose a suspicion and guilt about their new existence. Religious thinkers kept alive the doubt that genuine religion could thrive in the city. They saw the city as basically evil, or at least so immediate an occasion of sin that it did not deserve wholehearted approval.

The city was too secular, leading its residents in a hundred different ways to forget God and indulge in selfishness and idolatry. The sophisticated city dweller had no time for the smells and vulgarity of the shepherds. The technology of the city was superior to the grazing of sheep. Even in our own time, slang puts it this way: the city slicker will put the country hick in his place.

The Cain and Abel story is an image of this conflict. Abel, as the noble shepherd whose sacrifice is pleasing to God, represents the idealism of the pastoral community. Cain, the founder of the first city, is the anxiety-ridden symbol of urban life whose inability to truly worship God leads him to destroy his brother. The biblical text gives no reason why God preferred Abel's sacrifice to Cain's, but the readers of the original story knew well that it signified the abiding conviction that God could not be worshiped best in the city.

HOSTILITY BETWEEN ISRAEL AND JUDAH

The story also served as a symbol of the hostility that existed between the northern and southern kingdoms—Israel and Judah. Only for two brief reigns did the Hebrews know political unity. Under David and Solomon, all twelve tribes were united under throne and altar in Jerusalem. But no sooner was Solomon dead than a civil war broke out and the kingdom split apart (*see* page

CAIN'S MURDER OF ABEL *is a story with much greater meaning than the account of brother killing brother*

118). From that time on, the hostility between Israel and Judah became a matter of fact.

Judah, the less prosperous nation, considered itself the true Church, and Jerusalem the only true place to offer sacrifice to God. It chose David, the shepherd king, as its patron, and like Abel, was comforted in the thought that God would be pleased with its worship. Israel thrived economically, with its merchant princes making money from wars and natural resources. It entered into treaties with Syria to form a coalition to conquer Judah, and thus kill off its brother.

In the story of the Samaritan woman at the well of Jacob, she feels that Jesus would not consider worship at Gerizim, the holy mountain of the northern kingdom, pleasing to God (*see* page 223). In other words, Israel was Cain, in the minds of the southern kingdom. Israel was the alienated brother, fat with wealth and poor in faith.

FREEDOM OF RELIGION RECOGNIZED

One of the desert tribes that were neighbors to the people of God was the Kenites. It was traditionally held that they were founded by Cain. In some instances, Kenites lived in the same village with Israelites and were allowed freedom to worship their own god. Again the story of Cain and Abel appeared to be the background for this enlightened religious policy.

After Cain had killed Abel, he wandered "east of Eden." In his conversation with God following the murder, he felt so lost and alone that he thought he himself would be slaughtered by the first man he met. But God told him that any man who would touch him would be avenged by God Himself. " '. . . Not so! If anyone slays Cain, vengeance shall be taken on him sevenfold.' And the Lord put a mark on Cain, lest anyone who came upon him should kill him" (Genesis 4:15). So the Kenites and the Israelites lived in religious peace together in the same towns.

Others have seen in the story of Cain and Abel a mystical meaning. Noting that the Mass includes the sacrifice of Abel as a foreshadowing of the sacrifice of Jesus, they see, in the shepherd Abel, Jesus the Good Shepherd who not only offered a lamb, but was Himself the lamb offered. Abel acted as a priest in presenting the lamb of God. Jesus, too, was the high priest who Himself became the lamb offered to the Father.

THE STORY OF CAIN AND ABEL CAN
HAVE MANY MEANINGS

It may seem overdone to see all these meanings in this one story. But given the mentality of the people from which the story came, it is not so surprising. The Cain and Abel narrative is but one of a long series of artfully constructed stories which grew out of the centuries of contemplation of the community of faith.

It participates in the quality of great poetry in that it is open-ended and, therefore, justly able to be the vehicle for numerous depths of meaning. Growing out of the richness of the life of faith, a poetic narrative is like the ringing of a large bell in which the reverberations continue long after the first strike. It has resonance. This means it resounds many times in many hearts and many situations.

Hence, whether we have the original story of a jealous brother, or the rivalry of the brother kingdoms, or the sanity of religious tolerance, the Cain and Abel story is strong enough to bear all the meanings. It is fair to say that for our own very technical-minded civilization in which the poetic is neglected, such an approach to the Cain and Abel tale will appear unsuitable. But a little honest thinking about it, and a sincere acceptance of the world view of a culture far different from ours, can make it easier to accept.

We know that even today brothers and nations rise up against each other with murderous intent. Any newspaper bears testimony to that. The Cain and Abel story reminds us that such hatred is the outgrowth of sin and selfishness. This story also reminds us that we should strive to be our brother's keeper—that is, to have for him the love and concern of Jesus Christ so that we can replace this chaos of hostility in the world with love.

GOD'S CONSTANT CONCERN FOR MANKIND
The Story of Noah

On a television show the well-known comedian Bill Cosby brought renewed popularity to the old Noah story with his popular routine of Noah as a doubter and then as a hard-pressed suburban husband building the ark in his neighbor's driveway. With the true touch of the humorist, Cosby has found the human predicament in which Noah found himself: doubt in the face of the demands of faith, and harassment in trying to do what faith tells us we must do.

SAVED BY GOD FROM THE FLOOD

Noah ignored the mocking of his neighbors who thought the flood would never come. He completed the ark because he had faith that God would be true to His word. He must have felt somewhat silly building a ship on dry land with no water nearby. This test of Noah's is similar to the one which would face Abraham later on (*see* page 38). "By faith Noah, being warned by God concerning events for the saving of his household . . . built an ark" (Hebrews 11:7).

Noah was allowed to bring unclean animals into the ark, though not so many as the clean ones. In this we can see a rejection of those cults which were alien to God and which used such animals. Then Noah, his family, and the animals entered the ark, and God shut the door after them. Thus God sealed and protected His friends against the coming storm.

The accounts in the Bible about the severity of the flood vary. One account speaks of a forty-day rainstorm. "And rain fell upon the earth forty days and forty nights" (Genesis 7:12). But another account indicates a disastrous worldwide flood. The heavenly ocean above the skies broke through the firmament, and the ancient sea underneath the earth erupted through the land chasms. As a result, creation returned to chaos (*see* page 16). "I have determined to make an end of all flesh" (Genesis 6:13).

Not only were men and beasts destroyed, but the very earth itself. But God remembered Noah. God curbed the rush to chaos before Noah and his group were destroyed. And the ark began to find a resting place. The Hebrew word for rest is *nuah* which, as you can see, is a pun on the name Noah. In the faithful and heroic Noah, rest and peace began to return to the earth as the storm receded.

THE OLIVE BRANCH, SIGN OF NEW PEACE

It was a common custom among ancient seamen to send forth birds to test for land sites. Noah had no success with the first bird. It had to return. The second, a dove, was more successful; it brought back an olive branch in its beak. This olive branch of peace signaled the departure of angry judgment and the hope of deliverance. The third, also a dove, was sent forth and did not return. Then Noah knew that he could live again upon the earth.

The first thing Noah did after leaving the ark was offer sacrifice. Hence, the first human act on the liberated earth was an act of worship. This liturgical act celebrated the cleansing of the earth. So awesome was this moment that Noah remained absolutely

THE STORY OF NOAH *teaches us that God can never forget His world*

silent. God "smelled" the sacrifice and was pleased with the sweetness of the gift and with the men who offered it.

GOD PROMISED NEVER AGAIN TO DESTROY THE EARTH BY WATER

Then the narrator takes us to the secret thoughts of God. As he had shown a troubled God before the flood, now he notes a new attitude in the mind of the Lord. God is to take a new attitude toward men. This is not directly caused by His pleasure in the sacrifice—the author is always careful to protect the sovereign freedom of the Lord. But at least the sacrifice became the occasion for God's decision never to so punish the earth again.

God knows that man will continue to do evil. It was this that drew forth from Him the judgment of the flood. But now this very same condition becomes the occasion of God's grace and providence. He will try now in the face of man's stubborn sinfulness to bring him the saving grace.

GOD'S COVENANT WITH NOAH

Chapter nine of Genesis dwells on the covenant scene between God and Noah. The whole atmosphere was that of a new creation. Once again man was summoned to be fruitful and multiply. He would have control over the animal world and could kill animals for food. But God would retain the sovereign right over human life, though He gave man the right to punish a blood crime. "Whoever sheds the blood of man, by man shall his blood be shed" (Genesis 9:6).

Then God presented the covenant to Noah. Its purpose was to make clear the relationship that must exist between God and man. There was a difference between this covenant and the ones that would occur later with Abraham and Moses (see pages 42 and 71). For them, there was a direct personal call to enter the covenant, and, in a sense, God awaited their free decision. But here nothing was asked of man.

It was a covenant placed high above the earth. It was wrought out of the colors of the rainbow, a warm and promising assurance that God's grace would never be missing from the earth again. It was a rainbow covenant that kept men looking upward to the peace that comes after a storm, to a constancy that would never fail, to a gracious God who can never forget His world.

The Hebrew word from which we take the word "rainbow," ordinarily means a "bow of war." Hence, what the primitive Hebrews understood was that God had pledged to set aside His bow of war and not terrify the creation again with the threat of chaos. The appearance of the rainbow signaled the restoration of the order of nature. As God began to heal the universe, shutting off the ocean from above and the sea from below, He would continue His work of reconciliation in the stormy seas of the human condition.

The whole Bible is just such a story of God's breaking through to our awareness in every way possible, whether by the harmony of colors in the rainbow, the wholesome face of a child, or the broken bodies of the wounded. In countless ways God is always at work reconciling man to Himself through His Son, Jesus Christ.

GOD WILLS LIFE FOR ALL MEN
The Story of Abraham and Isaac

Many a modern dad may be tempted to become violent with his teenage son because of frustration over long hair, the up-beat dance, or an obedience problem. But that well-satisfied father, Abraham, had no problems with his son Isaac. Certainly, he would never think of killing Isaac. In fact, nothing could have seemed more absurd. Like the businessman who sees in his only son the hope of carrying on the family name and company ideals, Abraham saw that God's promises to him would be fulfilled through the survival of his son.

ABRAHAM PREPARES TO FULFILL GOD'S STRANGE COMMAND

The Bible attempts to relieve the anxiety of the reader by casually noting that this was only a test. Yet somehow the very idea of a father being ordered to kill his son drives the reader to nail-biting. We shall review the facts of the case and then draw some conclusions. (*Read* Genesis 22.)

In stark, matter-of-fact prose, the Bible describes how God told Abraham to take Isaac to Mount Moriah, and there knife the boy

ABRAHAM'S FAITH *remained firm though tested severely, and God rewarded him with the promise: "You shall be the father of a multitude of nations" (Genesis 17:4)*

and burn him as a religious sacrifice. With no comment on the disappointment or shock of the father, the text itemizes the preparations, almost as if they were getting ready for a fishing trip. They arise early. The servants are instructed to chop some kindling wood and saddle the pack animal for the journey. A little after sunrise the fated group – father, son, and two servants – sets out on the three-day journey to Mount Moriah.

ABRAHAM AND ISAAC ARRIVE AT THE PLACE OF SACRIFICE

Three days later they sight the well-known mountain, and Abraham instructs the servants to go home. The father and son walk on alone in a heavy, embarrassing silence. The boy carries the wood, not knowing it will be used to burn his own young body. The father carries the fire-making equipment and the knife. (The Hebrew noun could be accurately translated "butcher knife.") Only a few words pass between them during that journey. Isaac asks, "Where is the lamb for a burnt offering?" In answer, the old man simply says that God will provide the victim.

Now they arrive at the goal of their journey. The Hebrew text uses verbs here which give the impression of a dream, producing the mood of a robot or a sleep-walker carrying out orders. Abraham piles some stones together in a sort of crude altar bed, upon which he stacks the wood.

A VOICE FROM HEAVEN SPARES ISAAC

Then Abraham turns to his son, and ties up the apparently unresisting boy. Placing him on the altar, he raises the butcher knife in midair, ready to destroy his only hope. Only now is the tension broken, when a voice from heaven commands him to spare Isaac. "Do not lay your hand on the lad or do anything to him; for now I know that you fear God, seeing you have not withheld your son, your only son, from me" (Genesis 22:12). At this point Abraham notices a ram snagged by his horns in a nearby bush. He takes this animal and offers it to God in place of his son.

SACRIFICE OF THE FIRSTBORN COMMON IN ANCIENT RELIGIONS

What is the meaning of this strange story which seems to be cruel enough to scare a young child away from such a God, and to make all of us wonder if this is the sort of bloodthirsty deity to whom we should commit ourselves?

If we were to study other ancient religions, we would note the common practice of pagan rituals which demanded the sacrificial death of firstborn children. We would see in this story God's warning to Israel that He does not want such a practice among them. The Hebrew people were well enough aware of this custom of sacrifice, because it was common among their neighbors. Here are some texts illustrating the point:

"Then he [the king of Moab] took his eldest son who was to reign in his stead, and offered him for a burnt offering upon the wall" (2 Kings 3:27). "The Sepharvites burned their children in the fire to Adrammelech and Anammelech, the gods of Sepharvaim" (2 Kings 17:31).

Even Judah itself was guilty of such practices. Ahaz, king of Judah, "burned his son as an offering, according to the abominable practices of the nations whom the Lord drove out before the people of Israel" (2 Kings 16:3).

THE MEANINGS OF THIS STORY

James Michener, in his novel *The Source*, gives a vivid description of the details and the reasons why the ancients offered human sacrifice. Scientists examining the royal tombs at Ur in Mesopotamia found evidence of the ritual killing of children and substitute kings. But the story of Abraham and Isaac has a deeper meaning than the condemnation of human sacrifice done in the name of religion. Indeed three deeper meanings can be found in

GOD PROMISES ABRAHAM: *"I will make you a great nation; I will bless you and make your name so famous that it will be used as a blessing"* (Genesis 12:2)

this story: (1) God takes a long time to fully accomplish His will; (2) God wills life, not death, for all men; (3) God will provide His Son as the lamb of sacrifice.

Winning one fight does not make a prize-fighter. It is rare that an army wins a war in one battle. Abraham's journey to a new country and his patient waiting for Isaac's birth were the first trials to his faith. But these were not enough. The terrible test on Mount Moriah shows the depth of faith needed to accomplish God's plan. It also shows that His purpose will not be spelled out in one generation.

Furthermore, it shows that God is not on the side of death, but wishes life for all men. Prior to Christ's coming, Abraham could only know life after death through the survival of his son and descendants. God's rescue of Isaac from the edge of death is a forecast of the victory Jesus would have over death.

In this story a ram is substituted for Isaac, Abraham's son. In the New Testament, Jesus, God's Son, is the lamb that is sacrificed. It's not hard to see the similarities. In both cases we have the "only son" of the father. Isaac carries the wood up the hill, as Jesus carried the wood of the cross up Calvary. And both stories end with a new lease on life.

TRUST IN GOD IS MORE IMPORTANT THAN CLEVERNESS
The Story of Jacob

Esau and Jacob are the most famous set of twins in the Bible. Esau was nicknamed "Red" because of his complexion, while Jacob was called the "wrestler" for being so aggressive a rival of his brother. They were not identical twins in either their looks or in their likes and dislikes. Esau was an outdoor man, a hunter, and a favorite of his father, Isaac. Jacob, on the other hand, liked being around the house, and was much loved by his mother, Rebekah.

REBEKAH PLOTS TO GAIN THE INHERITANCE FOR JACOB

Isaac was growing very old and was making plans to transfer the family farm to Esau, the firstborn of the twins. He would do this at a ceremony called the "blessing." But Rebekah wanted Jacob to inherit the property and leadership of the family. She overheard Isaac discuss the blessing with Esau, and saw him send Esau off to hunt wild game to be used at the dinner preceding the giving of the blessing.

Rebekah, knowing that Isaac was blind and feeble, decided to deceive him. Right after Esau left, she roasted a lamb, using spices to make it taste like a game animal. She persuaded Jacob to wear some of Esau's smelly, old clothes, and she wrapped his neck and hands with animal skins. Then she built up Jacob's confidence so that he would not fear to "play the game," and deceive the old man.

JACOB GETS ISAAC'S BLESSING

It was a nervous Jacob who took the steaming meal into Isaac's room. Tense moments followed as a confused Isaac raised questions. He was surprised that the game had been caught and cooked so fast. Though the boy sounded like Jacob, he had the hairy skin of Esau and the musty smell of sportsmen's clothes. Isaac was satisfied after he had examined his son and had eaten the faked food. He gave Jacob the solemn blessing: "May God give you of the dew of heaven, and of the fatness of the earth. . . . Be lord over your brothers, and may your mother's son bow down to you" (Genesis 27:28–29).

Of course, it was a cruel blow to Esau to discover how he had been cheated out of his inheritance. He knew that the blessing, once given, could not be revoked. He threatened to kill his brother, and so thoroughly frightened him that the smooth-skinned Jacob left home for a few years. (*Read* Genesis 27:1–28:5.)

The young heir decided to go north and live with his uncle Laban's family. On the way he stopped at the pagan shrine of Bethel. During the night he had a dream about angels traveling to and from heaven on a giant ladder. God told him that his mission was to be like these messengers linking heaven to earth. (*Read* Genesis 28:10–22.)

JACOB MET RACHEL *at a well that shepherds used for watering their sheep*

JACOB COURTS RACHEL AND IS
TRICKED BY HER FATHER

The next event in Jacob's life was his meeting with Rachel. He had paused by a well, waiting for someone with a bucket to draw up the water. It was Rachel who came, and when they saw each other, it was a case of love at first sight. It turned out that she was a daughter of Laban, his uncle. She brought Jacob home and there followed a scene of welcome and rejoicing.

Laban hired Jacob to look after his sheep. In time Jacob asked to marry Rachel, promising to work seven years in return for the favor. Laban agreed, but secretly gave Leah, Rachel's ugly sister, to him instead. Her face was so heavily veiled at the wedding that

Jacob did not know that this was Leah. The disappointed bridegroom went to Laban and complained. Laban shrugged the matter off by saying that this was his only chance to palm off the homely girl. Then he shrewdly suggested that for an extra seven years of service Jacob could have Rachel. Jacob grudgingly agreed. (*Read* Genesis 29:1–30.)

JACOB OUTWITS LABAN

The years passed and Jacob served Laban well. Now he wanted to return to his own farm and bring his wife and family there. He had quietly begun to prosper during his years in the north as a result of a tricky bargain he had struck with his uncle. They had agreed that Jacob could keep any sheep that had black or spotted pelts. Since these would be so rare, Laban had little to fear. But according to the story Jacob had found a way of breeding that caused an unusual number of such sheep to be born. (*Read* Genesis 30:25–43.)

So Jacob started home with his family and friends and flocks. He heard news that Esau had become a desert prince over the neighboring tribe of fierce Edomites. What was worse, Esau and four hundred Arabs were riding toward his camp at that very moment—apparently to do him harm. (*Read* Genesis 32; 33.)

A WRESTLING MATCH: JACOB'S NAME IS CHANGED

That night, Jacob paced the field near the sleeping camp, wondering and worrying about what to do. While he struggled with his fears, a mysterious stranger came up and began to wrestle with him. The battle went on most of the night until Jacob's thigh was thrown out of joint.

The stranger said, "Let me go, for the day is breaking." Jacob answered that he would not do so until he received a blessing. Then the other man said, "Your name shall no longer be called Jacob, but Israel, for you have striven with God and men, and have

A **WRESTLING MATCH**: *the night Jacob wrestled with a mysterious stranger was the turning point of his life*

prevailed." After the stranger left, Jacob said to himself, "I have seen God face to face."

Now he recalled the danger which Esau presented. He sent servants and gifts to calm the oncoming tribesmen. The mission succeeded, and when the two brothers finally met, they embraced each other in forgiveness and love. With that, Jacob happily returned to his homeland and settled with his family and possessions.

GOD'S CHOICE OF LEADERS OFTEN PUZZLES US

This story raises a few puzzling questions. Why did God want the younger Jacob for patriarch instead of Esau? How could the Bible record the deception of Isaac by a future patriarch? What is the moral lesson taught by the cleverness of Jacob?

God chooses all men to receive His blessing. However, He chooses some men in a special way, so that through them He can make His love and mercy clearly known to all other men. The privileged man who is chosen in a special way has the obligation of being God's witness in a special way. More is expected from the man to whom more has been given. God often picks the unlikely candidate as in the case of Jacob, or in the story of the choice of David as king of Israel (*see* page 101). God is free to choose whom He wants. These stories illustrate this freedom.

MORE THAN CLEVERNESS IS NEEDED TO ACHIEVE TRUE SUCCESS

It does not seem very flattering to have Jacob cheat Esau out of the blessing, although the ancient peoples loved tales that showed the cleverness of a leader. God obviously did not approve of Jacob's action: He subjected Jacob to a lengthy penance for it at the hands of his uncle Laban.

The long night in which Jacob wrestled with the stranger was the turning point of his life. It was a night in which the conscience of the clever Jacob was purified. He learned that playing it smart is not as important as trusting in God. And so Jacob became Israel, the father of the twelve tribes.

A MAN OF FAITH
AND FORGIVENESS
The Story of Joseph

There is nothing like jealousy to ruin a family. Old Jacob favored his son Joseph, giving him expensive clothes to wear. His brothers stewed in envy because of this. Joseph gained the reputation of being a dreamer. The trouble was that his dreams were about becoming master over his brothers. So, his brothers had little love for him. They had reached such a point of dissatisfaction that they planned to kill him. But one of the brothers, Judah, persuaded them to sell Joseph to a passing caravan of Ishmaelites instead. They dipped his hated cloak in some goat's blood and told Jacob his beloved son was slain by a wild animal. (*Read* Genesis 37.)

JOSEPH ENSLAVED IN EGYPT

At the age of seventeen Joseph arrived in Egypt where he was sold as a slave to an Egyptian officer named Potiphar. Joseph became manager of this man's estate. Potiphar's wife fell in love with the handsome Joseph, but he would not return her love. This made her angry. One day when Joseph was alone with her

in the house, she made one last attempt to entice him. But Joseph
fled from the house, leaving his coat behind. She screamed for
help. That night she told her husband: "The Hebrew servant,
whom you have brought among us, came in to me to insult me;
but as soon as I lifted up my voice and cried, he left his garment
with me, and fled out of the house" (Genesis 39:17–18).

So Joseph was jailed. It wasn't long before his leadership talents
emerged, and he was put in charge of the other prisoners. One
day two important prisoners arrived, the butler and baker of the

Pharaoh. They had offended the Pharaoh and were sent to Joseph's prison. At night, wild dreams tore at their sleep and they awoke, puzzled men. Joseph noticed their tense faces and asked the cause. They confided their dreams to him.

THE BUTLER'S AND BAKER'S DREAMS INTERPRETED BY JOSEPH

The butler dreamed about a vine with fat grapes. In his dream he had taken the Pharaoh's cup and pressed wine from the grapes and presented it to the Pharaoh. Joseph said: "Within three days Pharaoh will lift up your head and restore you to your office; . . . But remember me, when it is well with you . . . make mention of me to Pharaoh, and so get me out of this house" (Genesis 40: 13–14).

The baker dreamed about a platter on his head. Three cakes rested on it. Then birds came and ate the cakes. Joseph hesitated to give the meaning. But the baker pressed him. So Joseph answered: ". . . within three days Pharaoh will lift up your head—

JOSEPH WAS SOLD *by his brothers to a group of Ishmaelites who were on their way to Egypt*

from you!—and hang you on a tree; and the birds will eat the flesh from you" (Genesis 40:19). Three days later the Pharaoh celebrated his birthday. He released his butler and brought him back as cup bearer. But the body of the baker swayed in the breeze underneath the gallows. The butler, however, did not remember Joseph.

JOSEPH INTERPRETS THE PHARAOH'S DREAMS

Two years passed, and now the Pharaoh had dreams that made him toss in his bed. He stood by the Nile watching seven fat cows grazing in the meadows. Suddenly, seven skinny cows came up and devoured the fat ones. He had a similar dream in which seven thin ears of grain swallowed up seven plump ones. He went to his counselors for an interpretation, but none of them could produce an answer. Then the butler remembered Joseph who had been so expert in explaining his dream in the prison. Pharaoh sent for Joseph.

The young Hebrew came into the royal court. He listened to the details of the Pharaoh's dream, and then gave his interpretation. "The seven good cows . . . and seven good ears are seven years . . . There will come seven years of great plenty throughout all the land of Egypt, but after them there will arise seven years of famine, and all the plenty will be forgotten in the land of Egypt. . . . And the doubling of Paraoh's dream means that the thing is fixed by God, and God will shortly bring it to pass" (Genesis 41:26–32).

PHARAOH APPOINTS JOSEPH TO PREPARE FOR THE FAMINE

The Pharaoh sat there wondering what he should do. Joseph advised him to build warehouses to store extra grain in preparation for the coming famine. He counseled him to appoint a secretary of agriculture to oversee the gathering of the grain and the building of storage warehouses, and to solve the distribution problems for the lean years. The monarch agreed that this was the best solution. He spoke to Joseph: "Since God has shown you all this . . . you shall be over my house" (Genesis 41:39–40). He invested Joseph with the proper symbols of his office — the Pharaoh's ring, a linen cloak, a gold neck chain, and a royal chariot.

For the next seven years golden fields of grain greeted the nation's eyes. Workmen built huge granaries to store the wheat. Then sharp winds and hot sun dried up the earth. The famine arrived. Over in Canaan, the family of Jacob saw their supplies of wheat running low, and began to worry. Travelers told them of the grain supplies in Egypt. They held a family council and decided that all the brothers, except Benjamin, the youngest, would go to Egypt to buy grain.

JOSEPH REUNITED WITH HIS FAMILY

The law required that those who came from outside Egypt had to check with Joseph for permission to buy grain. His brothers went to Joseph's office. The years had changed him so much, his brothers didn't recognize him. But he knew them right away. He asked them a lot of questions about his father and family. He wanted to know why Benjamin had not come. They said their father feared losing Benjamin as he had lost Joseph years before, due to their jealousy. Joseph demanded to see Benjamin, and held Simeon as a hostage.

They returned home with the grain and the bad news. Jacob grieved, but would not let Benjamin go. In time, however, as food became scarce, they faced the choice of starvation or bringing Benjamin with them. Jacob relented when his son Judah staked his life on saving Benjamin. (*Read* Genesis 42, 43.)

Joseph wept when he saw his young brother. He stood up before them and confessed: "Come near to me, I pray you . . . I am your brother, Joseph. . . . Do not be distressed, or angry with yourselves, because you sold me here; for God sent me before you to preserve life" (Genesis 45:4–5). Tears of joy rolled from their

JOSEPH IS MADE GOVERNOR *of Egypt by the
Pharaoh who gave him the symbols of his
new office: a ring, a linen cloak, a neck
chain, and a chariot*

eyes as the news sank in. Joseph invited them to come and live in Egypt, bringing with them his father Jacob. The old man received the news with joy, saying "It is enough; Joseph my son is still alive; I will go and see him before I die" (Genesis 45:28).

GOD CHOSE HIS PEOPLE FROM MANY NATIONS

Now we can see that, in a sense, God has chosen His people out of all nations. Abraham, from Mesopotamia; Isaac, from Canaan; Joseph, from Egypt. The theme of the third day, as in the dreams of the butler and baker, reflects death and resurrection. The baker died and the butler lived. The episode in the house of Potiphar makes Joseph a heroic defender of purity and a man faithful to the religion of his fathers. The reader delights in the test which makes his brothers uneasy, seeing it as a deserved penalty for their cruelty to him years before.

Some scholars used to worry about the truth of the story, for they could not see how the Egyptians would put a Hebrew in charge. They found no Egyptian historical records to support the work of Joseph. But now we know that about this time a fierce tribe of Semitic horsemen had overthrown the Egyptians and ruled Egypt for about two hundred years. They were called the Hyksos, or shepherd kings. As Semites, they would be sympathetic to a Semite like Joseph. When the Egyptians regained power they destroyed all records of this period. Hence, the absence of evidence.

GOD IS PRESENT IN THE STRUGGLE FOR FREEDOM AND JUSTICE

The Hebrews Delivered from Egypt

Revolutions make the headlines of history, They quicken the patriotism, the energies, and ideals of men, as the history of the American Revolution shows us, and as the struggle of minority groups for equal rights, here and elsewhere throughout the world, amply demonstrates. The Old Testament Hebrew revolt against the Egyptians followed the usual plan of revolutions. This fact should lead us to see that God is present to the revolutions that bring men a measure of human freedom.

REVOLUTION IS BORN FROM A CRISIS OF INJUSTICE

In the centuries after Joseph, the Hebrews were "fruitful and increased greatly" (Exodus 1:7). But the Hyksos pharaohs (*see* page 57) had been driven out and replaced by native Egyptians who had little sympathy for the Hebrew minority group within their boundaries. The new pharaohs considered the Hebrews a threat to Egypt. They believed that as the Hebrew population grew the danger to Egypt increased. The advisers of the Pharaoh, Rameses II (1290–1224 B.C.), told him he should (1) use the Hebrews as slave labor; (2) reduce the Hebrew birth rate.

Egypt kept many soldiers on her northern border to fight off invaders coming from the Gaza Strip. But she needed new supply depots closer to the front lines. Hence emerged plans to build the supply cities of Pithom and Rameses. Hebrew men were pressed into slave labor for the work. As for the babies, official Egyptian midwives were ordered to murder all newborn Hebrew boys. (*Read* Exodus 1.)

GOD PROVIDES A LEADER

God heard the cries of His people and raised up a leader to deliver them. Moses was a heroic man: he had a deep sense of justice, and had the courage and prudence needed in a leader who would fight against great odds. Instead of living a life of ease in Pharaoh's court where he had been brought up, he chose to share in the suffering of the people of God. (*See* Hebrews 11:25.) He received his official summons to be the rebel leader in a mysterious vocation scene before the burning bush on Mount Horeb. It was an awesome event in which God revealed Himself as mighty, consuming as fire, and compassionately interested in men. God thus placed Himself as the origin of the revolution. (*Read* Exodus 2.)

Aaron the priest was chosen to serve as a spokesman for Moses the prophet. The plan for the revolution was this. First, Moses would rally the people with speeches, stressing that departure from Egypt was the will of the God of their forefathers. Next, they would negotiate with the Pharaoh to seek a peaceful solution. Third, God permitted a series of national calamities to bring the Pharaoh to his knees. (*Read* Exodus 3–4.)

AIM OF THE HEBREW REVOLUTION: FREEDOM AND JUSTICE

Now Moses set the plans in motion. He stirred the people and strengthened their desire to be freed from a life of slavery. The negotiations with the Pharaoh failed. Hence began the famed ten plagues to pressure the Pharaoh into submission. (*Read* Exodus 7–12.)

Many efforts have been made to explain the ten plagues as just plain natural happenings. It is said that the bloody Nile is the result of red slag washed into the river during the spring flood. We are told that flood conditions normally produce swarms of frogs, flies, and lice. And hail storms and plagues of locusts are not unheard of. But this is to overlook the real meaning of the story: God is present at the heart of this revolution to bring freedom and justice to men. And He is not above using disasters to bring it about. These stories are not meant to be fairy tales. They are meant to show us the faith of the Hebrews, through which they knew that they would soon have their freedom as a result of these disasters that were weakening the power of the Pharaoh.

It is the final and most violent plague – the death of the firstborn – which marks a victory for the rebels. Pharaoh gives in to Moses: "Rise up, go forth from among my people . . . and go and serve the Lord as you have said. Take your flocks and your herds and be gone" (Exodus 12:31–32). (*Read* Exodus 12.)

THEY OWE THEIR FREEDOM TO THE WORK OF GOD

The Hebrews had, with God's help, succeeded in throwing off the old order, but this is not enough. The people must understand what kind of new order must come out of the chaos. In human terms, this means the people must now work responsibly to form a new community rooted in justice and freedom. In religious language, this means that people must see the new order as the arrival of the kingdom of God in their midst. It means they must

MOSES, *chosen by God to lead His people out of Egypt, had the courage and prudence needed in a leader who would fight against great odds*

never forget they owe their freedom to the work of the God of their fathers. It was no simple task to drill this into the people's minds, for even years later they wanted to return to the flesh pots of Egypt. (*Read* Exodus 13.)

In order to keep alive the memory of their deliverance and its meaning, the Hebrews celebrated a paschal meal once a year. During the meal, the events of the escape were recited, God was praised for His concern, and the people reaffirmed their faith in His continuing presence and interest in their needs.

ARE WE, LIKE THE PHARAOHS, HOLDING OTHERS IN BONDAGE?

The godly revolution in Egypt takes on greater meaning today when violent changes are taking place all over the world. Africa, Asia, and South America are brimful of people who feel oppressed, poor, hungry, and far behind their prosperous brothers in other parts of the world. The brush fires of revolt and resentment flare across these continents. The biblical story reminds us that these cries are like the groans of the Hebrews — and that God is listening to these new pleas.

It would be too bad if the rich Christian nations fail to recognize God's will that these people achieve freedom and justice. The African jungles are a new burning bush in which God is even now calling out for a leader to come and "let His people go." Out of the Christian people should come men with the bravery and insight of a Moses, unafraid to champion the cause of the poor, energetic in pursuing justice for the oppressed, and able to see the presence of God in the midst of these poor nations' struggle for equality with the rest of the world.

THE NEED FOR FAITH

The Hebrew revolt against the Pharaoh moved toward success after the tenth and most violent plague — the death of the first-born. Bearing the bones of the patriarchs, the Hebrews marched

toward the Sinai wilderness. The book of Exodus says that God
went before them by day in the form of a cloud, and at night in the
form of a pillar of fire. In other words, the Hebrew people understood that their true leader was God, glorious in the cloud and radiant in the fire. Not only was He their leader, He was also their
defender. Camped by the Red Sea for the night, the Israelites
turned in terror to see the Pharaoh's troops coming to bring them
back. But the pillar of fire stood between them and the soldiers
while Moses prepared the people to get ready to march into the
dark sea of death.

The Bible teaches that God wills life and freedom for all men,
but the price He exacts is a trusting surrender to the dark possibility of losing all. Abraham faced the dread of losing his son,
and in accepting that risk he not only saved his son, but also became the father of every man who has faith (*see* page 42).

This dire night, the Israelites faced the bleak prospect of marching into the waters. Timid and hesitant, they found it hard to
move. Moses stirred them to action. "Fear not, stand firm, and

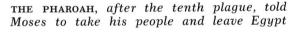

THE PHAROAH, *after the tenth plague, told
Moses to take his people and leave Egypt*

see the salvation of the Lord" (Exodus 14:13). Moses was not just trying to calm their fears. He wanted them to see that this whole event was an appearance of "God's time." In other words, they must see that God is present in this event, and that He is calling on them to have faith in Him.

ALWAYS OPEN TO THE FUTURE

Then God announced to Moses the words which have become the motto of the Church in pilgrimage even down to our own times. "Tell the people of Israel to go forward" (Exodus 14:15). With these words God asked Israel (and us) to always be open to the future, to say "yes" to the events that lie before us. God will march before them to reinforce His message that they are to be a pilgrim Church, and that they will find their life and freedom in this way only. (*Read* Exodus 14 and 15.)

In a beautiful Passover hymn, later composed to celebrate this event, Moses describes the astonishing wonders of that night: "At the blast of God's nostrils, the waters piled up. The floods stood up in a heap . . . but the people of Israel walked on dry ground in the midst of the sea" (Exodus 15:8, 19). Once the Hebrews arrived safely on the other side, the Egyptian soldiers came across in pursuit. And Moses recalls: "You did blow with your wind, and the sea covered them; they sank as lead in the mighty waters" (Exodus 15:10). Then Miriam, the sister of Moses, picked up a tambourine, and together with the other women began a victory dance by the shores of the Red Sea. "And Miriam sang to them: 'Sing to the Lord, for He has triumphed gloriously. The horse and his rider He has thrown into the sea' " (Exodus 15:21).

ISRAEL'S DELIVERANCE IS MARKED BY
THE FEAST OF THE PASSOVER

The Israelites were filled with awe and gratitude at the victory that the God of their fathers had achieved for them. They began to celebrate the memory of their deliverance from Egypt every year, and in time this celebration took the form of the Passover festival. This ceremony made present again to the minds of the Israelites the marvelous deliverance that God had accomplished for them in the past.

Here are some details of the meal. The lamb must be perfect, and not more than a year old. The head of the family killed the lamb, pouring its blood into a special hole dug at the door of their tent. In later history the slaying took place at the temple, and the blood was poured at the base of the altar — a symbol of the doorway to God's house. This was done just before sundown.

CELEBRATION OF THE EUCHARIST
IS THE NEW PASSOVER MEAL

Instructions called for roasting the lamb. Bitter herbs, made of lettuce, chickory, peppermint, snakeroot, and dandelion, were part of the menu. They symbolized the sufferings of Israel. Bread at the meal was dipped into a sauce, called haroseth, made of pounded nuts and fruit, sprinkled with vinegar.

The recital of the events of the night they escaped from Egypt was a sort of Bible service that strengthened the people's sense of God's saving presence in their own time and situation. The father of the family related the exodus event to the present situation of his own family, reminding them that God is always ready to bring deliverance to His faithful people. The idea of a word service being linked to the Passover meal has been carried over into our own Eucharist today in which a series of readings and prayers precede the sacrificial meal.

So we see in the Red Sea story an event and a Passover meal. The event was Israel's march to freedom. In time, the Passover meal took the form of a festival which would help Israel remember the Holy Night, and share in the dynamic power of God, manifested then and throughout all their history. In Christian times this event is the death and resurrection of Jesus. The Eucharist is the new Passover meal.

FAITH DEEPENED THROUGH TRIALS
The Israelites' Pilgrimage to Sinai

Freedom doesn't necessarily make a man a *man*. The magic age of twenty-one with its legal freedoms is not a guarantee that we have a real man on our hands. Freedom does not make a person mature. Freedom makes it possible for a person to gain maturity. The victory at the Red Sea brought the Hebrews freedom, but they still needed to grow up and find themselves as a people.

WOULD THE HEBREWS' FAITH GROW DEEPER?

The pilgrimage to Sinai, on which the Hebrews set out after their escape from Egypt, was a maturing process. It took faith to bring the people to an exodus triumph. But life must go on, and God wanted to see if their faith would grow deeper. The writer of the book of Exodus does not concentrate on the historical and geographical details. Like an artist brushing in the bold strokes on the canvas, the author cites a few of the stops on the way to Sinai. He chooses to dwell on the faith problem of these people.

The harshness is mentioned, but the details are few. Everything is streamlined to make the point: the saved Israelites were still subject to the same kind of struggle that all men meet in history. The big difference here is that revelation from God gives the real meaning of the struggle. The desert pilgrimage, with its fears and crises, conveys the teaching that Israel's faith, begun at the Red Sea, needs much deepening before final fulfillment. Hence, Israel must live responsibly in history. God saved Israel, but hunger, thirst, and enemies still abide. God tested them to see if they would live by the faith that had brought them this far.

THE SOUR WATERS OF MARAH

Water becomes all-important to desert travelers. Occasionally some of the desert springs turn sour for any number of reasons. The people complained to Moses that the wells of Marah were bitter. He dropped some wood into the water, following an old Bedouin solution to this problem. In so doing he was successful in sweetening the water. Moses taught the people that God was the healer of Israel, that the sweetening of the water was a sign of this. He reminded them that this was but the beginning of the challenges God would address to their faith. (*Read* Exodus 15:22–26.)

THEIR CONFIDENCE WEAKENS

Israel journeyed onward past the wells of Marah, coming next to the lush oasis of Elim, sheltered and cooled by seventy palm trees. The road over which Israel marched has been identified by modern scholars as an ancient highway built by the Egyptians for the purpose of easy communication between Egypt and the copper mines of the Sinai peninsula. Refreshed by the stop at Elim, the people picked up again, moving into a territory known as the Wilderness of Sin.

Weeks passed, and a heavy boredom set in. Bare rocks, bland food, and a dull sameness began to eat away the already frail self-confidence of the people. Their memories drifted back to Egypt's gardens, to the village markets crowded with meats and spices and fruits, to evening meals that filled the air with flavor. Their present problem was the more painful because they were tempted to a certain hopelessness. After all, where were they going? Was there really a goal to achieve? What kind of God would do this to them?

GOD'S GIFT OF MANNA, *a sweet breadlike substance, taught the Israelites to trust in the divine leadership*

THE GIFT OF MANNA

They came to Moses and laid their cards on the table. They made it clear that their morale was low, that the situation was worsening, and suggested that it might be better to return to the "flesh pots" of Egypt rather than rot away in despair. Moses took the matter to God in prayer. God's answer was the gift of manna. Underneath the tamarisk trees the people would find manna, a sweet breadlike substance that would remove the blandness of their diet and serve as a sign of the divine presence. "Each morning you shall see *my glory* in the appearance of the manna." The word "glory" in the Bible usually means striking evidence of the divine presence (*see also* pages 142, 299).

Manna, then, marks the presence of God. Its new arrival each day taught the people a growing trust in the divine leadership. In later centuries the book of Wisdom, recalling the manna story, taught that divine wisdom, like manna, brings pleasure to the heart of man. ". . . you did give your people the food of angels, and without their toil, you did supply them from heaven with bread ready to eat, providing every pleasure and suited to every taste" (Wisdom 16:20). In chapter 6 of the Gospel of John, Jesus speaks about the Eucharist as being the ultimate meaning of what was foreshadowed in the books of Exodus and Wisdom. And in the Lord's Prayer we say: "Give us this day our daily bread." This manna-wisdom teaching is remembered in every Benediction ceremony by the following versicle and response: "He has given us bread from heaven. Containing in itself all sweetness."

THE QUAIL

Coupled with the manna story is the narrative about the gift of quail, migratory birds from East Africa that used the Sinai peninsula as a landing strip for rest after their exhausting trip. "And there went forth a wind from the Lord, and it brought quails from the sea, and let them fall beside the camp. . . . And the people rose . . . and gathered the quail" (Numbers 11:31). It is curious, however, that the eleventh chapter of Numbers considers the quail incident a curse and not a blessing. "While the meat was yet between their teeth, before it was consumed, the anger of the Lord was kindled against the people, and the Lord smote the people with a very great plague" (Numbers 11:31–32). Some of the people died and were buried at that spot. The Bible's moral judgment is that their craving was unreasonable, and that such undisciplined desire can lead only to one's destruction. (Read Exodus 16.)

WATER FROM THE ROCK

The Israelites came to the oasis of Rephidim only to find the water supply had failed. Once again, the frayed nerves of the people showed how much maturing they needed and how thin was their trust in God. Their complaint was loud. God, like an exasperated father, advised Moses to strike a rock called Horeb. Out of it came a fresh stream of water. But the depth of the people's bitterness and the shallowness of their faith made Horeb's rock a monument to human fickleness and a testimony to God's fidelity.

It was at this spot that Joshua and a band of guerilla fighters had to ward off the attack of a Bedouin tribe led by a man named Amalek. The Bible notes that Moses kept his arms upraised in prayer, and that it was through his prayers that God awarded Israel the victory. (*Read* Exodus 17.)

These are but a few instances of the trials of Israel which somehow developed their faith and contributed to their maturity. They were a pilgrim people in quest of a deepening faith and a growing awareness of God's presence.

THE TEN WORDS
OF GOD
The Covenant at Sinai

Friends are not won easily. Friendship cannot be achieved overnight. God had set out to make friends with Israel. He began by demonstrating His saving power in Egypt. He took His people safely through the Red Sea. He provided them with signs of love and care during their pilgrimage to maturity. At the same time, He urged in them the growth of responsibility and self-determination. God now brings Israel to Sinai for what the Bible calls a covenant event.

COVENANT: A HANDSHAKE OF
TRUE FRIENDSHIP

A covenant is like the right hand of friendship, a clasp that cements relations. Today we would use the word covenant to describe a treaty or an agreement. The ancient world knew of two kinds of covenants. There was the covenant that took place between a powerful overlord and a relatively small and helpless neighbor. The powerful chief promised protection and other such benefits in return for loyalty, and perhaps a tax. There was also the covenant that took place between two kings of equal strength who imposed upon themselves mutual obligations. The covenant at Sinai was like the one between the overlord and the small and helpless neighbor. God was the powerful overlord who had delivered Israel from her enemies, who had lifted her up and helped her toward a sense of identity, and put in her the hope of becoming a holy nation and a kingdom of priests.

As a holy nation she would experience a certain separateness from other peoples. As a kingdom of priests she would have the mission of bringing the meaning of God to all the world. Israel's later history proved that she was unable to hold this balance of the holy and the priestly. On the one hand, she became insufferably ingrown and nationalistic. On the other hand, she went out to welcome the false gods of other nations and fell into the grossest forms of idolatry. Later, Saint Peter, in one of his letters, told the new Christian Church that it, too, should be holy and priestly, and hence should not repeat the error of Israel (1 Peter 2:9–10).

THE COVENANT AS A CONTRACT

Ancient covenants followed a special literary style. They opened with a passage that named the parties involved. This was followed by a historical prologue, which stated the advantages received by the lesser power from the overlord, such as military protection and financial assistance. This element is clearly seen in the following passage: "Thus shall you say to the house of Jacob, and tell the people of Israel: You have seen what I did to the Egyptians, and how I bore you on eagles' wings and brought you to myself" (Exodus 19:3–4).

The next element of the covenant was the obligations placed on the underling by the overlord. Again the Bible follows this pattern. "Now, therefore, if you will obey my voice and keep my covenant, you shall be my own possession among all the peoples; for all the earth is mine and you shall be to me a kingdom of priests and a holy nation" (Exodus 19:5–6). This text illustrates not only an obligation of Israel, but advantages she will enjoy should she

MOSES *received the commandments on Mount Sinai. God gives us the gift of salvation, and we respond by keeping the commandments as a sign of our gratitude*

choose to respond. The terms of her obligations will be expressed mainly in the famed ten commandments.

Ancient covenants, then, always recalled the favors bestowed on the underling by the overlord, and then went on to lay down what the underling must do in return. In like manner, the covenant at Sinai recalled the favors God had in the past bestowed on Israel, and then laid down what the Israelites must do in return: mainly, they must keep the ten commandments. Keeping the commandments, then, is really a gracious way of accepting God's favors. Thus, living a moral life would not be a burdensome task; it would be a sensible and reasonable reply to God's goodness.

It should be noticed that God saved Israel before asking her to keep the commandments. The word "saved" here means liberated. Israel knew salvation before agreeing to keep the law of God. We often hear that we must keep the commandments in order to be saved. But we must be careful not to think that we earn salvation by keeping the commandments. God first gives us the gift of salvation, and we then respond by keeping the commandments as a sign of our gratitude. We are first saved at baptism, which is symbolized by the redemption of the Israelites at the Red Sea. This salvation was actually achieved by the death and resurrection of Jesus.

We keep the commandments, moreover, as a sign of our resolution to remain in the process of salvation. Salvation at the Red Sea was not enough. The march to Sinai was not enough. For, even after the giving of the covenant and the agreement to live up to it, there still lay ahead of the Hebrews the journey to the promised land. Even after this, life went on, and Israel was expected to live up to the high standards agreed to at Sinai.

OUR SALVATION IS THE WORK OF A LIFETIME

For us, too, though salvation begins at baptism, it does not stop there. It is a process which develops over an entire lifetime. Keeping the commandments, then, is a covenant entered into at bap-

MOSES *on Mount Nebo bade farewell to Israel: he died before he could set foot on the promised land*

tism, deepened by the renewal of the covenant in every Mass, and brought to a climax at the moment of our own death, in which we most perfectly identify with Christ's cross.

The Hebrew text calls the commandments the ten *words* of God. In the Bible, God's word is first presented to us as something creative. The opening chapter of Genesis shows God fathering all things into existence by His word (*see* page 16). At Sinai, God speaks His ten words in order to bring into being a fresh creation, namely, His people. By His ten words, He forms them into a holy and priestly nation. His words describe the quality of the relation they are to have with Him.

They are to be a people who do not worship false gods, or kill or steal or offend God in any other way. These words of God resound in the minds of Israel and soak like oil into their bones. The prophet Hosea would describe this later on in terms of a lover speaking to the heart of his beloved (Hosea 2:14–15) (*see* page 173). In the New Testament, the ten words would find their fullest meaning, when Jesus required that love be the basic motivation of all law (*see* page 266).

THE PROMISED LAND
Joshua and the Conquest of Jericho

It is one of the ironies of history that the greatest Hebrew of the Old Testament never entered the promised land. Moses, who had been the fiery freedom fighter for Israel, died before he could set foot on the land promised to his people. But his old eyes were privileged to see the new land beyond the Jordan. On the eve of his death, his friends carried him to the summit of Mount Nebo from which he gazed on the hoped-for land of promise.

It was with this memory and this hope that Moses died, leaving the leadership to his trusted lieutenant, Joshua. "And Joshua the son of Nun was full of the spirit of wisdom, for Moses had laid his hands upon him; so the people of Israel obeyed him, and did as the Lord had commanded Moses" (Deuteronomy 34:9).

ISRAELITES HAD TO FIGHT FOR THE PROMISED LAND

It is generally thought that God simply handed over the land of Canaan to the Israelites. After all, He promised it to them. But as it turned out, the terms of the promise involved the personal bravery and skill of the people. They had to invade the country and conquer it. The books of Joshua and Judges are documents that preserve the accounts of the military conquest of the land of Canaan.

Sometimes it is hard to realize why they were so insistent on having land. The reason is that the Hebrews found themselves forming into a coherent nation. Without a land upon which they could settle and call their own, they would have had great difficulty in achieving identity and a place in history. Land gives stability to a people. Unless the Jews had this land, there would not be an Israel. Hence they saw in their successful conquest of Canaan the blessing of God allowing them this good earth as a gift.

JOSHUA THE GENERAL

Joshua emerges not so much as a prophet, but as a general. One of his first decisions was to send spies across the Jordan to scout the area around Jericho. They slipped into the city, took note of the defenses, and paused for a night in the house of a woman named Rahab whose rooms were joined to the walls of the city. During the night, police raided her place looking for the spies, because someone had alerted the king about the strangers.

Rahab hid the spies and sent the police away. When they were gone she made a deal with the spies that if their soldiers were successful in taking the city, they would spare her and her family. The spies assured her that she would be protected. They advised her to hang a red banner from her window, so that in the heat of battle the soldiers could identify her house and not harm it. Rahab is honored for her help to Israel by being mentioned in the family tree of Jesus as recorded by Saint Matthew. (*Read* Joshua 2.)

After the spies returned, Joshua gathered the people for the crossing of the Jordan. They solemnly formed into ranks and marched to the banks of the Jordan. The priests walked ahead of them carrying the ark of the covenant on their shoulders. As their feet touched the water, the experience of the Red Sea was repeated. The waters parted and the people crossed in comfort. Students of the Middle East waterways claim that from time to time landslides occur in the upper Jordan that temporarily check the flow of the river and so turn it into "dry ground." At any rate, the story is presented here to parallel the Red Sea crossing.

MOSES TOLD JOSHUA: *"Be strong, stand firm; you are going with this people into the land the Lord swore to their fathers He would give them"*

JOSHUA'S TWELVE MEMORIAL STONES
MARK ENTRY INTO THE PROMISED LAND

Joshua called for the building of twelve memorial stones to celebrate the long-awaited moment when the Israelites would set foot on the land promised to Abraham. As the paschal meal commemorated the liberation from Egypt, so these stones commemorated the liberation from the sufferings of the desert. At the paschal meal the children asked, "What does it mean?" Here the children asked, "What do these stones mean?" Joshua said the answer should be "You shall let your children know, 'Israel passed over this Jordan on dry ground' . . . so that all the peoples of the earth may know that the hand of the Lord is mighty; that you may fear the Lord your God forever" (Joshua 4:21–24).

THE TAKING OF JERICHO

Joshua's first and most famous conquest was the taking of the city of Jericho. The strategy was strange by almost any standard. Every day for seven days, the army, led by the clergy carrying the ark of the covenant, walked around and around the city in absolute silence. This silent mob endlessly circling the city must surely have been an unnerving sight to the inhabitants of Jericho. On the seventh day, to the accompaniment of the bone-piercing noise of the rams' horns, the walls came tumbling down, and Joshua's soldiers entered the city. As had been arranged, the family of Rahab was spared.

Kathleen Kenyon, a British archeologist, has uncovered most of the ruins of the city of Jericho. She has concluded that it is one of the oldest cities in the world, probably founded about seven thousand years before the birth of Christ. One of the levels of Jericho uncovered, which dates from the time of Joshua (around 1200 B.C.), seems to show evidence of an earthquake. As a result of these findings, some scholars have tried to connect the earthquake with the tumbling walls of Joshua. Whatever happened, the old ballad singers of Israel remembered the important fact that Joshua took the city, and did so with the aid of God. (*Read* Joshua 6.)

BRUTAL TREATMENT OF ENEMIES

There is a serious moral problem raised in the books of Joshua and Judges. It can be illustrated by this passage: "Then they utterly destroyed all in the city, both men and women, young and old, oxen, sheep, and asses, with the edge of the sword" (Joshua 6:21). This utterly brutal way of dealing with enemies has puzzled commentators through the ages. How could someone blessed by God do such a thing?

What we must recall is that Joshua and the people were men of their times, held to the customs that prevailed in morality and warfare then. Their barbaric views and primitive approaches to war are not meant to be an example to us. We are not supposed to justify what they did. It has been a tragedy that in the course of Christian history, these Joshua stories have been used to justify the killing of our religious foes. Joshua did not act wrongly when his actions are seen in the light of primitive ideas of what was right or wrong. But humanity has progressed since then, and morality has developed with it.

One other text that has plagued interpreters is the one concerning the day the sun stood still. "And the sun stood still, and the moon stayed, until the nation took vengeance on their enemies" (Joshua 10:13). Not realizing that this was simply a fragment of poetry from an old soldier's ballad, never meant to be literally interpreted, some commentators racked their brains looking for eclipses and so on.

The final chapters of the book of Joshua describe the dividing of the land for the twelve tribes. In chapter 24 there is a covenant scene similar to that at Sinai. As you read these old stories, keep in mind the mentality of the people of those days. In this way, the book of Joshua can have much inspirational and religious interest for us today.

HEROES OF ANCIENT DAYS
The Judges

Judges is a book that has little to do with judges. A better name for them would be saviors, for the Hebrew Judges were less concerned about using law to achieve justice than to seek restitution and a new way of life for the oppressed. These men emerge as the heroes of ancient days, closely tied to the period of conquest begun by Joshua. Generally, scholars speak of six major Judges and six minor Judges. To get the flavor of the book it is probably best to concentrate on two of them and make a passing reference to some of the others.

A RELIGIOUS MESSAGE: ISRAEL NEEDS A SAVIOR

Aside from the personalities which dominate the book, there is a noticeable religious message leaping out from every page. It runs in the form of a repeatable cycle. Israel finds herself in a state of moral decline. As a result, her enemies move in and conquer her, making slaves of the people. At this, she cries out for deliverance. God hears her plea and sends a judge-savior to bring her to freedom. Hence Israel identified her defeats on the plains of battle with her moral decay.

DEBORAH THE PROPHETESS

Out of the various colorful characters I shall pick Deborah and Samson to illustrate the work of the Judges. Deborah is like an Old Testament Joan of Arc. She first appears as a wise old prophetess, uttering her oracles under a sacred tree. Israel has fallen under the power of her enemies, and Deborah is approached for guidance as to what to do. Caught by the Spirit of God she says it is time to fight back. She chooses Barak as her general and plans to meet the enemy on the plains of Esdraelon, just below Mount Tabor, where years later the Lord would be transfigured before the apostles (*see* page 299).

As is often the case in biblical battles, the Israelites seem hopelessly outclassed. The enemy plans to use chariots with great blades curling out from the sides, so that when the rushing horses bring the chariots into the thin ranks of the Israelites, the effect will be that of a farmer's scythe cutting down a field of grain. Furthermore, the chariots are made of iron, and the soldiers are well-armored. And against these are the ill-trained, ill-equipped soldiers of Israel. They have no horses, no chariots; their spears have stone tips. Yet Deborah says they must fight and have confidence.

A HEBREW VICTORY

On the day appointed for the battle, as the troops got into position, a violent rainstorm broke out. The River Kishon roared over the banks in a flash flood and the field of Esdraelon was transformed into a bed of mud. The chariots were stuck in the mire; the horses reared in panic with every clap of thunder and arrow of lightning. The heavy-armored enemy weaved clumsily through the storm, unable to withstand the light-footed Hebrews.

The captain of the enemy, a man named Sisera, fled from the

battlefield. He went to the tent of a Hebrew woman called Jael and asked for refuge and food. She gave him some warm milk and soothed him to sleep. Then, with a barbarism that would be shocking in our times, Jael took a tent peg and drove it through the sleeping general's head (*see* page 81).

The fifth chapter of Judges records a song which Deborah is said to have sung at the victory celebration. Of the storm she chanted: "From heaven fought the stars, from their courses they fought against Sisera. The torrent Kishon swept them away. . . ." And of the deed of Jael: "He asked water and she gave him milk. . . . She put her hand to the tent peg and . . . struck Sisera a blow. She crushed his head . . . pierced his temple. He sank, he fell, he lay still at her feet." (*Read* Judges 5.)

SAMSON

Less horrible and more beloved is the story of Samson. Born of a family in the tribe of Dan, Samson grew up into a man of tremendous strength. His parents enrolled him in the fraternity of the Nazirites. The Nazirites were a group noted for their special dedication to the cause of God. They symbolized their dedication by never cutting their hair or taking a strong drink. According to the story, Samson's strength lay in the great seven locks of hair that flowed from his head.

The accounts of Samson illustrate both his sense of loyalty to God and a human weakness that made his strength count for nothing. He entered into a mixed marriage with a girl from Timnah, Delilah, only to find grief for his infidelity. Her wedding guests mocked his peasant ways and his inability to make up riddles. When he finally did make up a riddle, out of his experience of finding honey in the carcass of the lion he slew, his wife betrayed him.

The marvelous exploits, which show Samson burning a Philistine harvest with torches attached to three hundred foxes' tails, slaying a thousand men with the jawbone of an ass, and single-

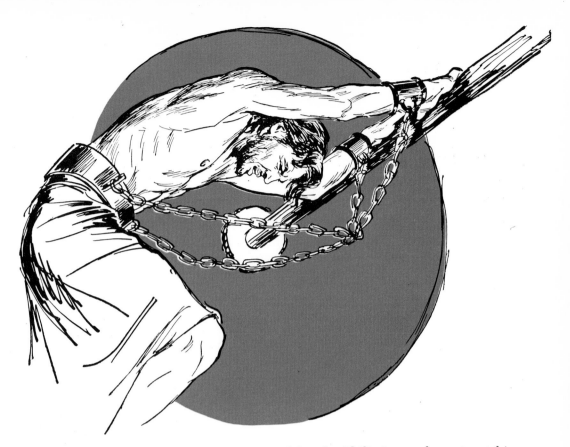

SAMSON *was seized by the Philistines, who put out his eyes and threw him into prison where he labored at grinding grain*

handedly breaking down the gate of the city of Gaza, are stories recalling how the Hebrews conquered Canaan.

SAMSON PROVES HIS FAITH

Samson's affair with Delilah has caught the imagination of poets, artists, and film makers. This account, wisely noting that even the most powerful of men can be tricked by the wiles of a woman, stands out as a uniquely human story. The loss of his hair signifies the loss of something much more important. He has been unfaithful to God. Samson resolves to make atonement for this. The return of his hair and his power accompanies the renewal of his faith. His destruction of the temple of Dagon, along with hundreds of people, symbolizes God's power, a power that can crush the false gods of Canaan. (*Read* Judges 13–16.)

THE JUDGES ARE INSPIRED LEADERS

Other Judges who achieved fame are Gideon, noted for his skill as a leader in conquering the Midianites, and Jephthah, who made a foolish vow to kill the first living creature he saw after a victorious battle: he planned to offer the victim as a thanksgiving sacrifice. Unfortunately, it was his daughter he met.

These heroic stories breathe of pioneer days. It is a time of battles and brutality. The Judges are leaders, inspired by the Spirit of God, who earned the respect of the tribes. In a sense, the whole state of the Hebrews at this time is somewhat freewheeling and bordering on complete disorder. It is precisely because of this sense of approaching anarchy that the people eventually make known their desire for a king, to get greater discipline and unity.

CHOOSING GOD'S WAY RATHER THAN OUR OWN

Samuel Solves his Problem: Saul Anointed King

Every great nation has its cast of heroes. The book of Judges preserves the thrilling story of the Israelites' dramatic rise to power. The period was a time of inspired leaders, a time of free-wheeling chieftains, warlords, and soldiers ready to fight for what they could get out of it. It is a textbook of wars aimed at illustrating a religious idea. The trouble was, however, that the independent chiefs seemed to have no sense of the need to unite more firmly. They did not realize that unless they united, total disorder would be the result.

SAMUEL'S PROBLEM

It was the last and greatest of the Judges who had the wisdom to notice the danger, and had the courage to take a painful step to do something about it. As a Spirit-filled Judge, Samuel was well aware that God had entrusted to him the destiny of the people. He was long familiar with the need to be sensitive to the divine presence. He was literally raised in a sanctuary, sleeping and dreaming each night beside the ark of the covenant.

During his early manhood, Samuel was engaged in military exploits like the other Judges before him. When he reached his declining years, he thought to make his sons serve as successors. But the elders of Israel felt that something more than the system of Judges was needed to keep the tribes from falling apart. "Behold you are old and your sons do not walk in your ways; now appoint us a king to govern us like all the nations" (1 Samuel 8:5).

This was the origin of Samuel's problem. It was not that he was so attached to pushing his own sons into the leadership. Rather, it was his lack of certainty. He was not sure whether it was a good thing for Israel to have a king. He knew that kings could bring much injustice in their time. And kings would naturally limit the freedom of the people.

SAMUEL'S COURAGEOUS DECISION

Samuel warned the people that the king would take the Israelites' sons and make them his horsemen; take their daughters to be perfumers and cooks and bakers; take a tenth of their flocks; make the people his slaves. Then Samuel told them, "And in that day you will cry out because of your king, whom you have chosen for yourselves; but the Lord will not answer you in that day" (1 Samuel 8:18).

Kings would take their freedom and make them forget God. In a kingdom the tendency to idolatry would be great. With Judges they would probably not forget God, and anyhow after a time Judges would probably disappear. Get a king and lose God. Keep the Judges and lose the nation. What was Samuel to do? Against his feelings urging him to save the old way, Samuel chose the kingdom.

The Bible does not describe the problem as clearly as I put it here. The biblical method is to place contrasting stories side by side. One story shows Samuel fighting to save the system of the Judges. Then another story describes him defending the need for the new kingdom and the efforts everyone must make to save the nation from falling apart.

THE SPIRIT OF THE LORD COMES UPON SAUL

In chapters nine and ten of the first book of Samuel, you will find the description of the process whereby Saul is chosen as king and the part Samuel played in this. You should note that Samuel speaks of the special action of the Spirit of God: "Then the Spirit of the Lord will come mightily upon you. And you shall prophesy" (1 Samuel 10:6). The reason for Saul's anointing of the Spirit is to show the people that he is truly one who represents God among them.

The people had become accustomed to having Spirit-filled men as their leaders. Hence, for the sake of a smoother crossing over from Judges to kings, this presence of the Spirit would be most useful. Revolutionary as the new order would be, it would not dispense with the obvious requirement that the leader should display the imprint of God. Not only was there an invisible anoint-

SAMUEL ANOINTS SAUL. *By this anointing the people are shown that King Saul represents God among them*

ing of the new king by the inrush of God's Spirit, there was also the visible anointing with oil.

SAMUEL CHOSE WHAT GOD WANTED — NOT WHAT HE WANTED

It is interesting that in chapter eleven of the first book of Samuel there is a different account of Saul's being chosen as king. Rather than being chosen by the Spirit of God or the wisdom of Samuel, Saul is chosen by the people because he has shown such courage and bravery in war, especially in the struggle with the Ammonites. This is a story preserved, not to sell short the work of Samuel, but to satisfy an understandable pride of a people who would naturally want to think their first king was a brave and worthy man.

The beauty of Samuel's solution to his problem is that he, an old man, broke away from the old way, which he himself preferred, and supported a new way of life for Israel because he loved her so much, and because he sensed it was what God really wanted.

FORGETTING GOD IN THE DRIVE FOR WORLDLY SUCCESS

The Story of King Saul

Saul, the first king of Israel, soon discovered that it isn't necessarily fun to be king. Samuel, the last of the Judges, never quite reconciled himself to the new order of things, even though he somehow knew this was the way things had to be. The Saul stories deal on the one hand with his military campaigns against the Philistines, and on the other with the problem of religion in a time of rapid social change.

THE CHALLENGE FACING SAUL

Saul knew he had to break the Philistines' control over the mining and production of iron. The Philistines controlled the mining of iron in Palestine, and so had an advantage over the Israelites. Saul knew that to overcome the Philistines he must train his men to be skilled troops.

At the same time, Saul was faced with the problem of religion in the new world he was creating. He was bringing Israel from the simple life of the shepherd to the complicated life of the town dweller. Now his people's simple faith was exposed to the dangerous religious practices of the Philistines. God was aware of these problems and sent the holy man, Samuel, to be the watchman of Israel during these troubled years of change.

SAUL CONDEMNED BY SAMUEL FOR OFFERING SACRIFICE

After his anointing, Saul's first big campaign was against the Philistines at Michmash. Saul was expected to make a sacrificial offering before going into battle, so that he would have God's blessing. However, the rite of sacrifice was reserved to Samuel. Saul, under pressure of the advance of the enemy, decided to offer the sacrifice himself. Samuel arrived at this moment and angrily condemned Saul for not waiting. "Obedience is better than sacrifice," declared the old Judge.

As the battle began, Saul commanded the soldiers to eat nothing until sundown. But his son, Jonathan, needed energy. He saw some honey and ate it. Saul heard of this toward evening and considered punishing Jonathan with death for his disobedience. Fortunately, Jonathan was bailed out by the soldiers who assured Saul that he had no need to be so strict.

OBEDIENCE IS BETTER THAN SACRIFICE

The Bible goes on to recount the second campaign of Saul against the Amalekites. Because this was to a certain extent a "holy war," Saul was expected to wipe out the city and every living thing in it. "Now go and smite Amalek, and utterly destroy all that they have; do not spare them, but kill both man and woman, infant and suckling, ox and sheep, camel and ass" (1 Samuel 15:3). This biblical equivalent of Hiroshima, an extreme of brutality difficult for us to understand (*see* page 81), was technically a religious holocaust. The Hebrew word for holocaust is *olah*. In religious services, the *olah* implied that the entire offering be consumed by fire and hence ascend in smoke to God. This is in contrast to the communion offering, in which part of the animal was saved and eaten by the people making the offering.

SAMUEL PRESENTS SAUL, *their new king, to the people, and they cry out "Long live the king!"*

Saul did defeat the Amalekites. "But Saul and the people spared Agag, and the best of the sheep and of the oxen and of the fatlings, and of the lambs, and all that was good, and would not utterly destroy them" (1 Samuel 15:9). So Samuel came again to rebuke Saul. The king defended himself by saying that he planned to use the good animals for a great sacrificial service of thanksgiving.

Samuel, never one to miss a dramatic possibility, broke out into a
poetic chant:

> "Has the Lord as great delight in burnt
>   offerings and sacrifices,
> As in obeying the voice of the Lord?
> Behold, to obey is better than sacrifice,
> And to hearken than the fat of rams"
>
> > (1 Samuel 15:22).

REDUCING A RELIGIOUS SERVICE TO MAGIC

The point at issue here, as in the incident at Michmash, is a
religious problem. It doesn't mean that sacrifice is unimportant,
but that it is useless if the inward disposition of obedience is missing. Don't bother offering sacrifice if you haven't first turned your
heart to God. King Saul, under the pressures of unifying the
tribes, building a nation, and breaking the Philistines' control over
the mining of iron, was reducing liturgy to magic.

This is all the more significant since Samuel's second condemnation takes place at Saul's encampment at the pagan shrine city
of Gilgal. The Philistines had established several well-known
shrine cities where elaborate sanctuaries were built to practice
idolatry. Some of the best known were Bethel, Hebron, Shechem,
Mizpah, and Gilgal. The fact that Saul was planning a sort of
merely efficient sacrifice, in a pagan sanctuary which had not yet
been purified by Israelite religion, partly accounts for the almost
excessive hostility of Samuel.

Samuel's religious theory was this: one must have a holocaust
of the heart before he can offer a liturgical holocaust. So strongly
did Samuel believe this, that he resorted to the extreme measure
of taking the kingship away from Saul's family: no son of his
would ever sit on the throne of Israel. The situation seems un-
usually cruel to us in the light of Saul's deeply humble efforts at
repentance and his plea for forgiveness. "Now therefore, I pray,

pardon my sin and return with me, that I may worship the Lord"
(1 Samuel 15:25). Saul desperately clung to the robe of Samuel
and even tore a piece from it. Samuel, however, was unmoved.
He looked at the piece of cloth in Saul's hand and told him this
was a sign that the kingdom would be torn from his family.

DAVID SPARES SAUL. *David, pursued by King Saul
and his soldiers, crept up to the king's tent unseen,
and though he could have killed Saul he merely cut
off the hem of his cloak*

A BROKEN AND TRAGIC KING

After this, Saul's career spiraled downward. Samuel anointed
David to be his successor. This brilliant young lieutenant achieved
striking military victories and charmed all the people to his side.
Saul's final years were filled with deep depression and black
moods. He was jealous of David, and felt deeply the ingratitude of
a people who gave him little credit for the breakthrough he made
against the Philistines.

Saul was better on the field of battle than he was by the lamps of the sanctuary. As happens to many men, he allowed his drive to get things done to obscure his religious principles. He produced an efficient war machine, but compromised his God in the process. He died a broken and tragic king.

Fortunately, David was not blind to Saul's greatness, and lamented him saying:

> "Saul and Jonathan, beloved and lovely!
>   In life and death they were not divided;
> they were swifter than eagles,
>   they were stronger than lions"
>   (2 Samuel 1:23).

A GREAT HUMAN BEING
The Story of King David

Almost any nation would be proud to include David in the list of its leading public figures. He was a shepherd, a poet, a warrior, a statesman, a lover. He was grateful and perceptive enough to know that his wide-ranging success depended a great deal on the spadework of Saul, from whom he inherited a disciplined army and people, and a clearer idea of the role of religion in the new nation.

DAVID'S FIRST TASKS

After his anointing at the shrine city of Hebron, David understood that his main missions were: to overcome a few who, with the help of Saul's family, still opposed him; to search for a neutral city to serve as a capital; and to establish a shrine around which could be built the religious fervor of the people.

Chapters three and four of the second book of Samuel preserve the accounts of David's unhappy task of overcoming the remainder of the house of Saul. The followers of Saul centered their hopes in the son of Saul, Ishbosheth, who was a hapless and ineffective leader. Ultimately he was beheaded by two assassins as he lay in his bed. They, in turn, were executed by David. This may seem gross ingratitude to us, but we must remember that Saul's son shared in the privileges granted to those whom the Lord had anointed. Only God could punish them for wrongdoing. David always kept this in mind in his treatment of anointed men of the Lord.

The fifth chapter describes how David took the Jebusite stronghold of Jerusalem. This mountain fortress seemed so safe from all attack that its defenders taunted outsiders with the remark: "All we need are the blind and the lame to ward you off." But David was a shrewd general, not easily put off by smooth walls and remarks such as this.

He discovered that the water supply for the city was hoisted from a tunnel deep in the mountain. David calculated: "Whoever would smite the Jebusites, let him get up the water shaft to attack the lame and the blind" (2 Samuel 5:8). By sending his soldiers into the tunnel and up the water shaft, David took the city.

In selecting the neutral city of Jerusalem, David avoided causing jealousy among the tribes. By moving the government offices away from Hebron, he gained a certain independence from the lobbying of any one tribe.

ARK OF THE COVENANT BROUGHT TO JERUSALEM

Now David had a religious problem to solve. Samuel had warned the people that the coming kingdom would make them "like all the nations." But Israel was supposed to be different from the nations, for they were the elected community of God, called to be a people of faith, abiding in His strength rather than in a totally human endeavor. Israel had a mission to be holy and priestly, not to be just another Oriental kingdom.

In the days of the Judges (see page 82), the religious ardor of the nation was sustained by the abiding glory of God that rested

DAVID, *at Hebron, became King of Israel as well as Judah. "At Hebron he reigned over Judah seven years and six months; and at Jerusalem he ruled over all Israel and Judah thirty-three years"* (2 Samuel 5:5)

on the ark of the covenant. Wherever they went the ark of the covenant went with them, impressing on them the supreme importance of their religion. But now that their nation had achieved stability, it was necessary to find a new way to centralize and make effective the rulership of God in Israel.

David's solution is found in the sixth chapter of the second book of Samuel. He reasoned that since he had established a political center in Jerusalem, why not have a shrine to crown the work of the state? He would bring the ark to the city and there build a permanent temple to house it. State and Church would stand side by side in friendly partnership. The kingdom would be served and God given His due glory.

The journey bringing the ark to Jerusalem was marred by the sudden death of Uzzah, who put out his hand to save the falling ark when the oxen pulling the wagon stumbled. Seen in context, his death was a way of instructing people in the need to preserve a reverential distance from the awesome God. In our age, when awe and wonder are no longer so closely connected with the divine and in which God is rarely associated with revenge, this story may have less meaning. Nevertheless, it should serve to remind us that this sense of awe and wonder should be preserved in every age.

DAVID DANCES BEFORE THE ARK

A second scene that captures our attention is the dance of David before the ark. It is hard for people today to link dancing with liturgy, but this was not the case in biblical times. It was only natural to take one's whole body and leap and sway with it rhythmically to praise the living God.

Some Bible commentators have seen in the procession of the ark a model of the procession of Mary to the house of Elizabeth. Mary, as the New Testament expression of the ark of the covenant, stayed three months in the house of Elizabeth, just as the old ark rested in the home of Obededom. As God rested upon the ark, so His Son rested within Mary.

THE ISRAELITES THOUGHT OF DAVID AS THEIR SHEPHERD

David solved the basic challenges of his life by establishing a centralized government crowned by the Church through the presence of the ark. His son, Solomon, would build the temple. Many colorful stories surround the figure of David, for instance, his struggle with Goliath and his historic friendship with Jonathan. These and other stories about David in the Bible show him to be one of history's great human beings.

The Israelites liked to think of David as their shepherd. Israel remembered the days when they were a tent community, enjoying the freedom of being on the move, experiencing the deepening of their relationships, and sustained in hope by the glory of God always marching before them. This is something David understood well since he himself had been a shepherd before entering public life.

THE BIBLE'S PRAYER BOOK
The *Psalms*

For some reason we don't ordinarily picture a soldier writing Church poetry. But that is exactly what the warrior King David did. He did not write all of the 150 psalms, but so great was his influence on the composition of psalms, that the book of Psalms has borne his name ever since. The psalms are prayers, but people today find it hard to really think of them that way. Here are some considerations that might be helpful in understanding the psalms.

HE WHO SINGS PRAYS TWICE

Saint Augustine says that he who sings prays twice. It is too bad that most people regard the psalms as a text to be read silently. The psalms are the songs of faith: war chants, victory songs, enthronement anthems, hymns about nature. In the shadow of the temple, fraternities of musicians gathered to compose melodies for the psalms.

There has been a recent revival in psalm singing, prompted by the work of Father Joseph Gelineau, a French priest-musician. The growing popularity of the guitar will no doubt have an impact on the singing of psalms, not just because David used a stringed instrument, but because it suits the vigorous rhythm of the words and the excitement of the situation.

ISRAELITE POETRY

The poetry of the Israelites is somewhat different from our ordinary idea of what poetry should be. There is no rhyme nor fixed rhythm in the sense we would normally expect. It's true that the free verse movement has given us a broad idea of what poetry can be. Israelite poetry might be summed up in the saying: never say anything once that you can say twice, and better still, three times. The rhythm of the psalms is a rhythm of ideas. In the following examples see how the second line parallels the idea of the first:

> "May God be gracious to us and
> bless us
> and make his face to shine upon us,"
> (Psalm 67:1).
> "Let God arise, let his enemies
> be scattered;
> let those who hate him flee before
> him!"
> (Psalm 68:1).
> "All the earth worships you;
> they sing praises to you,
> sing praises to your name" (Psalm 66:4).

The rhythm of the poetry of the psalms is a rhythm of ideas. An idea is stated and then repeated with different shades of meaning. It is the balanced drumming of a declaration that arises from the heart of a man who has known the miracle of God and now speaks out of the ecstasy of response. The psalms are the result of the experience of miracle and ecstasy. By miracle we mean the appearance of a mighty act of God, such as the Red Sea victory;

by ecstasy we refer to the joyous, human faith-experience of this work.

THE PSALMS CELEBRATE EVENTS AS MIGHTY ACTS OF GOD

It is true that we in the Western world love to reason, but this love need not exclude poetic experience. The psalms indeed revel in such vivid images as: mountains that dance, seas that howl like animals, clouds that ride in the sky as noble horsemen of God, and

JERUSALEM, *the city King David chose as his capital and site of the shrine that would house the ark of the covenant*

lightning that writes like a pencil God's presence into the hollows of the earth. When we can admit that these descriptions are real and not just fanciful ways of talking about God, we can accept the message of the psalms.

It was characteristic of the Israelites to find the presence of God in nature and history. It was the unique privilege of the Israelites to see and know that God was really doing something in this world. It has, after all, always been His world, but it takes a long time for many to admit it.

We owe a tribute to Israel for being perceptive enough to know that the events of nature and history were not just simple happenings, but the very acts of God. In the psalms we see that the Israelites had the original insight into God's presence in the movement of history. Put in another way, it was the Israelites who really were the first ones to see the divine purpose in history. As they saw the unfolding of historical events, they came to understand their history as salvation history. They learned to attribute these events to the presence of God.

THE PSALMS ARE ROOTED IN REAL LIFE

It is not necessary to use the psalms directly as our own prayers. After all, we certainly have the right to celebrate the presence of God in new words and in new ways. Yet the psalms do hold a privileged position in the history of prayer. They serve to show us how to pray.

They show us that in singing our prayer we are totally involved in it and yet lifted out of ourselves. They show us that poetry and symbols in prayer lead to the throne of God. Finally, they show us that all prayer reflects real life. The psalms are not lofty, otherworld prayers, but are rooted in the shouts, tears, smiles, and noises of a real world. Psalms are a theological commentary on the life of the people who sang them. Any prayers we compose should also be a result of our careful insight into our own world and its triumphs and tragedies.

REAL LIFE SHOULD BE WOVEN INTO PRAYER

Modern prayer that imitates the psalms should celebrate technology, sports, war, peace, love, home, and death. Real life should
be woven into prayer. A good example of modern prayer is given in
a fascinating book entitled *God is for Real, Man* by Carl F. Burke.
This book shows what happens when delinquent boys from
the city streets are asked to retell the Bible stories and rewrite the
psalms so that they have meaning for their lives. We need both
the ancient nobility of the psalms and a brisk modern meaning.
Out of the two will come a balanced approach to prayer in our
time.

THE TEMPLE IS BUILT AND DEDICATED

Solomon: High Priest and King

If Rome gloried in the memory of Caesar, Israel rejoiced even more in the memory of Solomon. He was Israel's equivalent to Louis XIV, France's "Sun King," though in many ways nobler and wiser. His father, David, was the romantic poet and warrior, while he emerges as the shrewd administrator and wise man. Palace plotting almost kept him from the throne, but the prompt intervention of his mother Bathsheba saved the day.

SOLOMON'S PRACTICAL WISDOM

Solomon's first decrees swept away all major pockets of opposition to his rule. The priest, Abiathar, who had supported forces hostile to Solomon, was put under house arrest in the sleepy, clergy town of Anathoth several miles north of Jerusalem. With no remorse, Solomon had General Joab executed right at the altar of sacrifice. It was Solomon's opinion that Joab's brutal and uncalled-for murder of Abner was deserving of capital punishment. (*Read* 1 Kings 2:28–35.)

Having pretty well cleaned house, Solomon turned his attention to the problems of organizing the nation. In his early years he was a deeply religious man. This was fairly well manifested by his prayer for wisdom and the energy he devoted to the building of the temple. He quickly saw that no Oriental monarch could survive without a large fund of practical wisdom. Life in the palace and the nation had a much better chance of survival if it took advantage of the heritage of practical wisdom that circulated in the courts of Egypt, Babylon, Syria, and Phoenicia.

It was Solomon's particular genius to combine his study of such wisdom with his faith and obedience to God. His prayer for wisdom shows he believed that the greatest wisdom of all was that which led men to godly devotion. (*Read* 1 Kings 3:1–9.)

THE PEOPLE DISTRUSTED CITY LIVING

Solomon's greatest achievement was the building of the temple, or as the Bible puts it: establishing the name of the Lord. The decision to build the temple was no light matter from either a religious or a technical point of view. For Israel, God was never in any fixed place. He moved with His people. As a pilgrim people, Israel was always moving forward to richer pastures and a better future. And God marched with them into that future.

Those who were caught up in this religious view of the divine presence feared that fixing a permanent abode for the ark of the covenant would take the power and movement out of their religion. Religion to them had overtones of a church on the move. Israel would always think of its nomadic days in the desert as the ideal time.

The Israelites had the uneasy suspicion that once they settled down into town life they would somehow be stained by urban living. They had, at first, a basic mistrust of the city, feeling that it promoted sinful living. It took away their sense of change, movement, and adventure which they had known in their desert wanderings. Their previous contact with cities introduced them to the immoral religious practices of the Canaanites. Actually, the story of Cain and Abel reflected this opposition between the pastoral Abel and the founder of the first city, Cain (*see* page 28).

THE TEMPLE SYMBOLIZED THE COVENANT WITH GOD

Now the fixed temple and the stabilized shrine of the covenant both stilled the mood of change and adventure, and reminded them of the civic shrines of the Gentiles. Solomon, however, wanted to show them another way of looking at the temple. He knew that, in time, they would become accustomed to city life and learn to celebrate the creative possibilities which such a life has to offer.

As a shrine the temple would illuminate the sense of covenant which God had established with David and his successors. Finally, the temple stood at the top of Mount Zion (or Sion) as a prophetic purifier of the State. Not that the temple itself could purify, but its very existence was a solid reminder that the divine presence brooded over the city and the nation. It was God who truly ruled the nation from Mount Zion and who raised up men to stand before the kings and governors and the wealthy, to call them to deal justly with the people and support a high standard of morality. (*Read* Isaiah 1:10–17.)

The architecture of the temple was an occasion of concern for the conservative and devout Israelite. Building fashions at the time were set by the commercial cities of Tyre and Sidon on the coast of Phoenicia. Solomon hired Phoenician architects and construction engineers to handle the building of the temple. Many a devout old Jew looked with puzzlement and wonder at the top of Mount Zion where he saw a building styled like the pagan sanctuaries used by the Canaanites. It seemed at first too secular, too profane, and not at all worthy of their God. But in time they came to accept it and eventually to glory in it.

SOLOMON, *when his magnificent temple had been completed, planned a great celebration, during which the priests would place the ark of the covenant in the Holy of Holies*

SOLOMON *hired Phoenician architects and engineers to handle the
building of the temple*

THE TEMPLE IS DEDICATED

Solomon's prayer at the dedication of the temple (1 Kings 8)
parallels his prayer for wisdom, and implicitly offers a few ideas
for the understanding of public worship:

>Liturgy begins with the official arrival and presence of God's
>glory.
>
>The gathered community is called by God.
>
>Their high priest and king recites the mighty works of God.
>
>In a litany of intercession he gathers up their prayers.
>
>The liturgy is climaxed by a sacrificial meal that celebrates
>the works of God and the faith of the people, and opens them
>in hope to the future.

After the clergy had placed the ark in the temple, the cloud-radi-
ance of God's presence came and filled the temple. It was so awesome that the priests could not stay within the temple walls. This

is a way of showing that liturgy officially is begun by God. The people who gathered around the building are called *qahal* in Hebrew. This is a word that indicates they are a "community called by God." They stand at the place of worship because they have a vocation to do so from God Himself. The worshiping community is one that is both summoned and formed by God.

SOLOMON: HIGH PRIEST AND KING

Solomon, as high priest and king, assumes the role of the old patriarchs who were accustomed to preserving and reciting the splendid works which God had performed for His people. As king. Solomon summarized and announced the memory of the community. This was designed both to reinforce the people's sense of identity and to sustain an attitude of straightforward gratitude in them. The litany of intercession expressed the abiding dependence of the Israelites on God and a renewal of their trust in the covenant.

The sacrificial event proclaimed the people's desire to praise God, to live in total dedication to God as shown by the holocaust of the lamb, and to have new hope in the future as they ate of the holy food. These elements of presence, recital, litany, gathered community, and sacrifice are themes that govern our own liturgy today. Read the story of the dedication of the temple (1 Kings 8) to renew and refresh your understanding of liturgy. In this event Solomon reached a summit of spiritual grandeur.

THE NORTH BREAKS AWAY FROM THE SOUTH

Two Kingdoms: Israel and Judah

Apparently even the wisest of men can make the most absurd errors. Solomon's early career was a brilliant mixture of practical administration and devoted service to God. He built a splendid temple to illustrate his conviction that real religion should unify the spirit and thought of a nation. At the height of his career, his counseling talents were sought by world leaders. The queen of Sheba graded Solomon as the wisest man in the world.

THE STAGE IS SET FOR TROUBLE

But into this paradise of wisdom crept the old temptation — to use human wisdom, not as a stairway to the stars, but as a means of satisfying our desires. Solomon found it was no simple matter to have an ambitious building program. He needed vast sums of money and a large labor force to build the temple and all the government offices now needed. Therefore, he taxed the people heavily. It is true that he took in great sums of money from foreign trade; but, since this was not enough, he resorted to slave labor. This practice was quite common in Mesopotamia and Egypt, but was fiercely resented by the Israelites.

Nothing in the Bible texts seems to indicate that Solomon imposed any new taxes on his own people of Judah, but this is because the tax and slave labor policy more than likely had been introduced in Judah by his father, David. This is indicated both by the census David took, and by the rebellion of Absalom who represented the dislike of the people for this system.

Solomon organized the northern tribes into districts for taxation and the draft. The twelve tax districts of Solomon did not correspond to tribal lines; in fact, Solomon deliberately tried to dissolve the old tribal ties in order to attach the people directly to the throne. He failed in this. The discontent that this caused contributed much to the civil war that followed his death.

SOLOMON'S MARRIAGES AND IDOLATRY

We shall now consider Solomon's second mistake. The Bible tells us that "King Solomon loved many foreign women. . . . He had seven hundred wives, princesses, and three hundred concubines" (1 Kings 11:1, 3). This is probably an exaggeration, but it does offer a clue to the grand style in which he lived. That he was able to marry an Egyptian princess showed both to what height Israel had ascended and to what a state of weakness Egypt had descended.

Solomon's marriages eventually led him to the support of idolatry. It may be of some interest here to note that idolatry and adultery are the same word in Hebrew. "For when Solomon was old his wives turned away his heart after other gods. . . . For Solomon went after Ashtoreth the goddess of the Sidonians, and after Milcom, the abomination of the Ammonites. . . . Then Solomon built a high place for Chemosh the abomination of Moab, and for Molech the abomination of the Ammonites, on the mountain east

DAVID *on his deathbed told Solomon, his son: "Be strong, and show yourself a man"*

of Jerusalem. And so he did for all his foreign wives. . . . And the Lord was angry with Solomon" (1 Kings 11:4–9).

AFTER SOLOMON'S DEATH THE CRISIS GREW

Even before Solomon's death the signs of coming trouble were apparent. Hadad, the prince of Edom, was hired by the Egyptian pharaoh to make life difficult for the aging king. The desert brigand, Rezon, established an independent kingdom at Damascus that became in time a serious threat to the kingdom of Israel. A group of prophets persuaded Jeroboam to initiate a rebellion against Solomon's slave policies. It was not a successful attempt, and Jeroboam was exiled to Egypt.

Idolatry, burdensome taxation, and a humiliating slave policy marked the corruption of Solomon's last days and fostered the kind of unrest that led to civil war after his death. Speaking of his death the Bible notes simply: "And Solomon slept with his fathers, and was buried in the city of David his father; and Rehoboam his son reigned in his stead" (1 Kings 11:43).

With Solomon dead, the crisis of disunity in the kingdom surfaced. The enthronement of the new king, Rehoboam, was to take place at the old sanctuary of Shechem. The leaders of the northern tribes summoned Jeroboam back from Egypt to represent their grievances to the new king. "Your father made our yoke heavy. Now therefore lighten the hard service of your father and his heavy yoke upon us, and we will serve you" (1 Kings 12:4). King Rehoboam asked for three days to study the problem before he would reply. He went into conference with the elders, who knew his father well. They counseled moderation, a mild answer, and the promise to live as a servant of the people.

REHOBOAM INSULTED THE NORTH: A NEW KINGDOM IS FORMED

Then Rehoboam had a meeting with a council of ambitious young men who had grown up with him. They urged the king to take a hard line: rather than cut back on taxes and slavery, increase them. Rehoboam decided to follow the advice of the young hard liners. Three days later, at a meeting with Jeroboam and the northerners, this harsh statement was made by Rehoboam: " 'My father made your yoke heavy, but I will add to your yoke; my father chastised you with whips, but I will chastise you with scorpions' " (1 Kings 12:14). At that, the northern tribes angrily left the conference, and declared that they would break off from the south and form a new kingdom to be called Israel. From then on, the southern kingdom would be named Judah.

The political break between the north and the south was accompanied by a religious one as well. The northerners set up a center of worship on Mount Gerizim to rival the sanctuary in Jerusalem. Centuries later, at the well of Jacob, Jesus talked about these two sanctuaries with the Samaritan woman (*see* page 223). The civil war tore the nation apart both politically and religiously. Since few things are more likely to divide people than religion and politics, it is easy to see why the Jews and Samaritans hated each other with a passion. It is also why Christ's story about the good Samaritan was so challenging to His Jewish listeners later on.

For our own day, the religious schism between Israel and Judah is a painful reminder of the division between Christians in our own time. Israel and Judah knew the tragedy of religious disunity, and yet there was the shining light of prophecy in both churches. But further, their religious quarrel turned them in upon themselves, and they thus lost their sense of mission to the Gentiles. Today's search for unity among the Christian churches provides a healthy contrast to the story of the fighting of brothers in the book of Kings.

THE TWO KINGDOMS DECLINE
Sin Destroys Nations

The Hebrews, once one nation, were now divided into the northern kingdom of Israel and the southern kingdom of Judah. The books of Kings tell how each of these kingdoms became sinful nations, abandoning God, practicing idolatry, and sinking into total decline. The Bible writers make it clear that sin directly caused the disorder and decline in which these kingdoms ultimately found themselves. At this time it would be helpful to review some of the notions that are included in the Old Testament idea of sin.

SIN IS A PERSONAL MATTER

Scripture sees sin as a *personal* matter. Sin is not so much the breaking of an abstract rule, than it is a breaking of a personal relationship with God. The Lord confronts Adam about eating fruit from the forbidden tree in the Garden of Eden. God summons Cain to the bar of judgment for murdering his brother, Abel. God sends the prophet Nathan to King David to point a nagging finger at the monarch, accusing David of adultery.

THE STORY *of the expulsion of Adam and Eve from Eden shows that sin is a break in mankind's relationship to God*

SIN IS SEEN AS PART OF A SERIES OF EVENTS

Second, in the Old Testament sin is never considered alone and apart from what comes before or follows it. Read the book of Judges to note the cyclical style in which sin is portrayed. "And the people of Israel did what was evil in the sight of the Lord and served the Baals; and they forsook the Lord, the God of their fathers, who had brought them out of the land of Egypt; . . . So the anger of the Lord was kindled against Israel, and he gave them over to plunderers, . . . and he sold them into the power of their enemies. . . . Then the Lord raised up judges, who saved them out of the power of those who plundered them" (Judges 2:11–16).

The cycle includes: a gift from God, the refusal of this gift by the people, the punishment of the Lord, the people's cry for mercy, and the appearance of God's redemptive power.

Third, sin narratives often conclude with *redemption symbols* or *savior figures*. After the sin of Adam comes the seed of the promise of a savior. Cain is saved from despair by God protecting him by means of a mark on his forehead. The dread waters of the deluge that washed away the world's sin give way to the optimistic rainbow that signifies God's intent not to harm the earth again. The exodus and Calvary events are the ideal saving moments in sacred history. Samuel, David, and Isaiah are among the savior figures which abound in the Bible. This emphasis on salvation all through the Bible keeps us from viewing sin in a purely negative way—something for which we are bound to be damned.

SIN IS A REFUSAL TO ACCEPT THE SALVATION GOD GIVES US

The books of the prophets commented on the sins of the people as recounted in the books of Kings. Whereas Deuteronomy concentrated on the *collective* sinfulness of the nation, the prophets shifted attention to the *individual* guilt of each person, inferring that sin lies in the hearts of men—men who are free and responsible human beings. The main conclusion of these writers is that sin is a refusal to accept God's saving work, and that this is seen in Israel's failure to measure up to the covenant standards set by God, and to which the chosen people had pledged themselves (*see* page 72).

These ideas are helpful for seeing the meaning of sin. They make us recall the personal character of sin. They broaden our outlook, enabling us to see sin in the cycle of grace, fall, cry for mercy, and redemption. They put sin on both a collective and an individual basis, relating it to a refusal of redemption and a failure to measure up to the divine standards to which we freely commit ourselves.

THE BIBLE'S HISTORY OF SIN

The biblical history of sin can be seen in two broad patterns. The first is the Adam pattern as seen in the primitive history given in chapters 1 to 11 of Genesis. The pattern is repeated in the story of the formation of Israel from the time of Abraham to the exile.

The Adam cycle includes the fateful event of Adam and Eve, the story of Cain's murder, the savagery of Lamech, and the account of Noah and the deluge. The story of Adam and Eve shows that sin is a break in mankind's relation to God. Within this account of the Garden of Eden is found God's initial offer of love and grace to men. Sin is the refusal to accept this gift and its gracious Giver.

The account of Cain's murder illustrates that sin also breaks the relationship between man and man. It not only affects the divine-human contact, but puts us out of touch with our fellowmen. Hence sin has disastrous consequences in the social order. Sin also spoils our control of the earth and our management of the land. Adam will no longer till the earth in comfort and confidence. He must sweat over it. The earth will be resistant to man unless he uses it for the sake of others. "Now the earth was corrupt in God's sight, and the earth was filled with violence" (Genesis 6:11).

The rest of the Genesis story tells of the gradual decline of the world. Men begin to deal with each other ruthlessly, as indicated by the savage chant of Lamech: "I have slain a man for wounding me, a young man for striking me. If Cain is avenged sevenfold, truly Lamech seventy-seven fold" (Genesis 4:23–24).

Sin has consequences that affect man's relation to God, to his fellowman and to the earth itself. Sin projects mankind into a hopeless loneliness that wrings from man an anguished cry of despair: "My punishment is greater than I can bear. Behold, you have driven me this day away from the ground; and from your face I shall be hidden; and I shall be a fugitive and a wanderer on the face of the earth, and whoever finds me will slay me" (Genesis 4:13–14). These words of Cain are as good an interpretation of the effect of sin as can be found.

God's ultimate weapon against sin is twofold. By the deluge, He will destroy all those who do not measure up to His plan. By the ark, He saves the family of Noah, the only just group on the earth. This salvation-damnation movement is found all through

THE STORY *of Cain's murder of Abel shows that sin not only breaks man's relationship to God but also the relationship between man and man*

the Bible. After the deluge, God begins a new creation, calling men and animals forth from the ark to start a new way of life.

GOD'S GRACE CAN OVERCOME SIN

The original sin of mankind repeats itself in the original sin of Israel. God graciously delivers the Israelites from the darkness of Egypt, and brings them into the symbolic Garden of Eden of the desert, where bread falls from heaven and waters spring forth from the rock. He gathers His people at Sinai for the covenant event, only to find that they forget Him and worship the golden calf. As Adam refused God's love symbolized by Eden, so now Israel rejects His love typified by the saving exodus and the gifts of the desert. Chaos and deluge followed the sin of Adam and the same happens to Israel.

The story of the Judges illustrates Israel's problem with idoltary. The history of the monarchy demonstrates the progressive worldliness of Israel amid tales of murder, civil war, strife, adultery, diplomatic intrigue. The history ends with the fall of the monarchy, the slaughter of the people, the burning of their cities, and the enslavement of the remnant in the Babylonian exile (*see* page 134).

Still, God kept alive the promise of redemption. Savior-figures crowd the pages of Israel's history: Moses, Joshua, Samuel, David, Josiah, and Isaiah. The Babylonian exile is like the deluge, but the faithful remnant live together as in an ark, sustained by the hopeful sermons of Ezekiel and the other prophets until Cyrus pronounces the joyful deliverance and return to the promised land.

Though sin crouches at man's door, God's grace is greater. This is the encouraging and optimistic teaching of the Bible and the corrective to the tragic decline of the two kingdoms.

A FERVENT AND FIERY PROPHET
The Prophet Elijah

It has been said that history is written by the victors. It is also often true that history is the account of kings and their court intrigues. In the light of this, it is refreshing to see in the books of Kings a six-chapter biography devoted to a local hero, the rugged and fiery prophet Elijah.

Elijah crashes onto the biblical stage like a bolt of lightning and exits in a fiery chariot. The only other prophetic figure who might outmatch Elijah is the venerable Moses himself. In the series of Elijah stories the colors are bright, the emotions volcanic, and the noise like the shouting at a spirited football game.

ELIJAH IS CALLED TO PURIFY ISRAEL

Following the death of Solomon, the Hebrew people broke apart into the kingdoms of Israel in the north, and Judah in the south. Both nations progressively declined into political and religious anarchy. Elijah entered Israel's history at the time when Ahab ascended the throne. Ahab married a pagan girl from Sidon, named Jezebel, built a temple of Baal for her in Samaria, and allowed her to install a community of four hundred pagan clergy in the capital city. "Ahab did more to provoke the Lord, the God of Israel, to anger than all the kings of Israel who were before him" (1 Kings 16:33). And God called Elijah to purify the kingdom.

ELIJAH BRINGS A DROUGHT TO PUNISH KING AHAB

Elijah stormed into the palace of Ahab and announced that for the next three years no rain would fall in Israel. The drought was designed to touch the conscience of the king and bring him to repentance. The prophet retired to the brook Cherith beyond the Jordan. It was by that fast disappearing stream that the series of legendary wonders which surrounded Elijah's career began. To satisfy his hunger, God sent ravens every morning and evening with meat and bread for the prophet.

When the stream dried up, Elijah went to the village of Zarephath where he obtained lodging with an old widow and her young son by paying rent with a miraculous supply of oil and meal. ". . . 'The jar of meal shall not be spent, and the cruse of oil shall not fail, until the day the Lord sends rain upon the earth'" (1 Kings 17:14). Some weeks later the little boy died, but Elijah raised him from the dead after receiving a proper scolding from the widow: ". . . 'What have you against me, O man of God? You have come . . . to cause the death of my son!'" (1 Kings 17:18).

When the three years of drought were up, Elijah returned to King Ahab and demanded to meet with the priests of Baal. The terms of this contest are worthy of the publicity stunts of a Hollywood press agent. Elijah and the priests were each to take a bull, put it on an altar, then pray that their respective god would send down fire to consume the animal. The scene of this strange encounter would be on the beach near Mount Carmel. To the victor would be given the "privilege" of slaughtering the defeated.

THE PROPHET ELIJAH *condemned King Ahab for taking posses-sion of Naboth's vineyard (1 Kings 21:17–29)*

GOD'S POWER IS TESTED IN A STRANGE CHALLENGE

The scene that day must have been like a sports event, with the spectators lining the hills as though in a grandstand. Elijah insisted that the priests of Baal have the first try. All morning long they filled the air with magic chants and psalms. Their bodies became more and more frenzied as they did one ritual dance after another around the animal offering. By noon they were barely limping. Elijah began to mock them: ". . . 'Cry aloud, for he is a god; either he is musing, or he has gone aside, or he is on a journey, or perhaps he is asleep and must be awakened.' And they cried aloud, and cut themselves with swords and lances . . . until the blood gushed out upon them . . . they raved on . . . but there was no voice . . . no one heeded" (1 Kings 18:27–29).

Then it was Elijah's turn. He ordered an altar built of twelve stones, representing the number of the Hebrew tribes. Next he demanded that a huge trench be dug around the altar. Wood was placed on the altar and the animal offering was laid carefully upon the wood. And there were spectacular details. Elijah instructed the people: " . . . 'Fill four jars with water, and pour it on the burnt offering, and on the wood,' . . . And the water ran round about the altar, and filled the trench . . ." (1 Kings 18:33, 35).

THE ALMIGHTY GOD APPEARS AS A CONSUMING FIRE

Then with superb dignity, summoning up in himself all the faith of Israel, Elijah prayed: "O Lord, God of Abraham, Isaac, and Israel, let it be known this day that you are God in Israel. . . . Answer me, O Lord, answer me!" (1 Kings 18:36–37). With that, a great fire came from heaven and consumed the burnt offering, the wood, the stones and the dust, and licked up the water that was in the trench. This brought the crowd to their knees with the fearful chant: "The Lord, he is God; The Lord, he is God." But Elijah wasted no time. He shouted: "Seize the prophets of Baal!" And they were captured and executed on the beach at Carmel. (*Read* 1 Kings 18:39–40.)

But these extraordinary events were not enough to change the heart of Queen Jezebel. She promptly sent out the royal police to arrest Elijah. Disgusted, frustrated, and disappointed, the prophet went away to the wilderness and sank in despair under a broom tree. His comment rose from an empty heart: "It is enough; now, O Lord, take away my life; for I am no better than my fathers" (1 Kings 19:4). He sank into a merciful sleep. On awakening, he found a loaf of bread and a jug of water by his side. He refreshed himself and looked up and saw an angel who commanded him to go forth and meet the Lord at Mount Horeb. And for forty days and forty nights he marched, sustained by the bread of God he had eaten under the broom tree.

THE VOICE OF GOD AGAIN SHOWS ELIJAH THE WAY

Elijah climbed the mountain and waited. Soon a hurricane wind shook the hills. This was followed by an earthquake. Then came a fire that baked the rock. But the Bible notes that none of these violent happenings manifested the presence of God. It was in the gentle breeze that followed these events that the voice of God was heard.

The Lord spoke to Elijah and directed him to anoint Hazael as king of Damascus, Jehu as the king of Israel, and Elisha to be Elijah's personal successor as prophet. This appearance of God at Mount Horeb, which is sometimes called Sinai, restored the prophet's strength. He went forth and did what he was told. He foretold the downfall of Ahab and Jezebel, especially condemning their unjust stoning of Naboth and the stealing of his vineyard (*Read* 1 Kings 19:13–21; 21).

Elijah's career ended with the passage of his cloak to Elisha and his ascension into heaven in a fiery chariot. Elijah's great vocation

ELIJAH'S *strange contest with the priests of Baal was intended to show forth the power of the one true God*

was to restore the purity of the covenant. This is why so many details of the life of Moses, the great covenant figure, surround the history of Elijah. The ravens that fed Elijah in the desert are like the manna in the exodus account. The conquest of the prophets of Baal recalls Moses' single-handed attack on the worshipers of the golden calf. The restoration of Elijah's strength at Mount Horeb (Sinai) recalls the covenant mediated by Moses at

Sinai. But it is interesting to note that Moses saw God amid the thunders of Mount Sinai, while Elijah met God in a gentle breeze on the same mountain.

ELIJAH'S FERVOR HEARTENED GENERATIONS TO COME

Figures as heroic as Elijah deserve more space than can be given here. May it suffice to note that Elijah loved Israel and attempted to save the kingdom, realizing that religious and moral corruption would dissolve the nation. He had temporary success, and his fervor sustained the faithful among the chosen people for generations afterward.

GOD PUNISHES JUDAH
The Babylonian Exile

The seeds of destruction planted by the follies of Solomon and the division of the nation that followed his death resulted in the fall of the kingdoms of Israel and Judah. Great prophets like Elijah tried to save the northern kingdom, but the effort ended in disastrous loss of hope.

The great prophets, Isaiah and Jeremiah, strained to bring Judah to repentance, but their sermons went unheeded. It is true that there was a temporary reform under good king Josiah, but it was too little and too late. The powerful forces of the Babylonian king, Nebuchadnezzar, were gathering as God's avenging arm against His faithless people.

WHY JUDAH WAS DESTROYED

The Bible assigns a religious reason for the destruction of Judah. "Surely this came upon Judah at the command of the Lord, to remove them out of his sight" (2 Kings 24:3). Jeremiah, in his famed temple sermon, outlines God's indictment against His people. He accuses them of theft, murder, and adultery, while hypocritically coming to worship at the temple. They rob defenseless widows, throw orphans into the streets, greedily grub for land, and then piously shroud their injustice with incense before the altar of holocausts. "The children gather wood, the fathers kindle fire, and the women knead dough, to make cakes for the queen of heaven [a pagan goddess]; and they pour out drink offerings to other gods, to provoke me to anger" (Jeremiah 7:18).

Over the mountain of Topheth, they threw their firstborn sons and daughters into the fire to placate a false god. Immorality, hypocrisy, and idolatry were common among the covenant people. Jeremiah literally shouts: "Be appalled, O heavens, at this, be shocked, be utterly desolate, says the Lord, for my people have committed two evils: they have forsaken me, the fountain of living waters, and hewed out cisterns for themselves, broken cisterns, that can hold no water" (Jeremiah 2:12–13).

ISAIAH'S CALL TO REPENT GOES UNHEEDED

Isaiah repeated the same ideas in his biting speech about liturgy in the first chapter of his prophecy. He comments on the great crowds that flock to the temple offering huge numbers of sacrificial animals, faithfully attending the festivals at the time of the new moon. Isaiah claims that God hates all this. He will not look when they spread out their hands to Him, nor will He listen to the multitude of their prayers, "your hands are full of blood" (Isaiah 1:15). Unless they cease to do evil, seek justice, correct oppression, they will be devoured by the sword (see Isaiah 1:17, 20). A hypocritical liturgy offered by a wicked people is a sign of the end fast approaching Judah.

But the people's ears were deaf and their hearts were corrupt. So in the reign of King Zedekiah, Nebuchadnezzar, the king of Babylon, came and laid seige to Jerusalem. Zedekiah and his men fled the city but were caught by the enemy and slaughtered. Then Nebuzaradan, the captain of the king of Babylon's bodyguard, began the systematic destruction of the city of Jerusalem. The Babylonians burned the temple, razed the palaces, and tore down the city walls. They took the bronze and gold of the temple and melted it down as part of the booty to be taken to Babylon. All Jews who were capable of any kind of skilled labor were chained and taken captive to Babylon. "But the captain of the guard left some of the poorest of the land to be vine-dressers and plowmen" (2 Kings 25:12).

JEREMIAH MOURNS FOR THE CITY

The fall of the holy city signaled the end of an era. It was a tragedy which was especially heartrending to a great prophet like Jeremiah. He loved his city and his land with the emotion of a patriot and the heart of a saint. He captured the mood of his own and the national grief in the mourning poems known as the lamentations. "How lonely sits the city that was full of people! . . . She that was a princess among the cities has become a vassal . . . my eyes flow with tears . . . my soul is in tumult, my heart is wrung within me. . . . Hear how I groan; there is none to comfort me" (see all of Lamentations 1).

It may seem strange that a prophet who was so fiercely critical of Jerusalem should now mourn so deeply over the city's destruction, until we remember that his criticism flowed from a genuine love for his people. The lament of Jeremiah is similar to the feeling expressed by Jesus about the holy city when He predicted its coming judgment. "O Jerusalem, Jerusalem, killing the prophets and stoning those who are sent to you! How often would I have gathered your children together as a hen gathers her brood under her wings, and you would not" (Matthew 23:37).

EXILED TO BABYLON

The seventy years of Babylonian exile was a time of purification. As Samuel had foretold, the monarchy would be a way of life that would turn the people away from honoring God as their true king (see page 88). The monarchy did, however, serve the useful purpose of creating a national unity that was not possible under the

JEREMIAH *mourned for Jerusalem as it lay in ruins, for though he had criticized the city his criticism flowed from a deep love of its people*

tribal confederacy. Prior to the monarchy, the tribes tended to be independent of one another and could have dissolved into chaos without the unifying factors brought to bear by the political possibilities of a monarchy.

But, in turn, there was a weakness in the monarchy in that the prosperity it brought and the idolatrous influence of other nations dimmed the people's memory of the covenant and turned their

hearts to other gods. Their prosperity was often achieved by injustice to the weak. Their idolatry arose from fascination with the
gods of other nations. Babylon was the fire that would purge out
corruption and idolatry.

The prophets, however, strove to keep alive the exiles' hopes
for the future. Jeremiah wrote a letter to the exiles that is astonishing, both for its practical advice and its optimism. "Build houses
and live in them; plant gardens and eat their produce. Take wives
and have sons and daughters. . . . But seek the welfare of the city
where I have sent you into exile, and pray to the Lord on its behalf,
for in its welfare you will find your welfare . . . nor be dismayed, O
Israel; for lo, I will save you from afar, and your offspring from the
land of their captivity. Jacob shall return and shall have quiet and
ease. . . . In the latter days you will understand this" (*see* Jeremiah
29:5-7; 30:10-24).

The Babylonian exile makes it clear that God will bring destructive judgment upon the sinful. There is no sentimentality here.
Evil men will be punished. "They slew the sons of Zedekiah before his eyes, and put out the eyes of Zedekiah, and bound him in
fetters, and took him to Babylon" (2 Kings 25:7). But there is always the hope of Noah's rainbow that God will not forget the
promise that he made to Abraham and to his seed. This is the hope
that sustained the Babylonian exiles. It is the same hope which
must hearten our Church today.

OLD TESTAMENT PROPHETS
Three Ideas About the Messiah

Old Testament prophets were busy men. They hastened between royal court and temple pulpit; they attended closed-door briefings on foreign affairs, and had their moments of repose alone with God. They had the unpleasant role of being professional critics of the State and of the Church. Yet they possessed the personal joy of divinely supported insight into the meaning of the public affairs of their day. Their hearts were anchored in the assurance that they were God's mouthpieces for the community of faith.

THE PROPHET'S FUNCTION

The name prophet comes from the Hebrew word *nabi* which means something like "mouthpiece." A prophet was God's voice trumpeted throughout the hills and cities of Israel. Prophets summoned kings and peasants to repentance, cursed politicians who led Israel into idolatrous alliances with foreign powers, and blessed the people with the hope of a messianic "day of the Lord."

While the prophets' main task was the religious interpretation of the contemporary events of history, they also made pronouncements about the future. It is as foretellers of the future that prophets are generally remembered, even though this was really a small part of their task. It is easy to understand how this attitude came about.

The early Christian Church was faced with the problem of urging the Jewish community to accept Christ. Hence much of the theological thinking centered around material showing how the Old Testament supported the possibility of Christ's being the Messiah foretold by the prophets. This is why the theologians of the apostolic age mined the prophetic writings for every kind of text which demonstrated the messianic mission in Christ's life. And, admittedly, the life of Jesus finds remarkable prophetic defense. The writings of the prophets are rich with material that identifies the characteristics of the messianic age and the Messiah Himself.

THE IDEA OF A MESSIAH

The idea of a Messiah grew out of the dissatisfaction of the prophets and the people with the given state of affairs. Present sorrow nudged them to a hope of better things to come. From the time of King David until Christ, three major messianic pictures emerge. Some saw the Messiah as a king, others as a suffering servant, and, finally, a few envisioned him as a man from heaven with a divine mission. The idea that the Messiah would be a king was popular during the times of the monarchy. God had made a covenant with King David, promising him that his throne would never die out (see 2 Samuel 7:4-17). As the years passed, with Judah experiencing one bad king after another, good men yearned for another King David, a messianic figure who would set things right.

Toward the end of the monarchic period, Judah did have two fine kings, Hezekiah and Josiah, but it soon became clear that neither measured up to the stature of a Messiah. Isaiah's famous prophecy of the Messiah being born of a virgin (Isaiah 7:14) was

THE PROPHET ISAIAH, *addressing King Ahaz, prophesies the coming of a king of David's line through whom God would be decisively with His people. This hope expressed by Isaiah was realized in Christ*

in the context of a Messiah seen as a king. The same is true of his poem about a Messiah who would rise out of the root of Jesse (Isaiah 11).

THE SUFFERING SERVANT

However, after the fall of the monarchy, the numerous sorrows that attended the Babylonian exile and the miseries experienced after the exile caused a sadness that Judaism found difficult to shake. Thoroughly disenchanted with the monarchy, the nation licked its wounds caused by the selfishness of its kings. It was no easy matter to revive the idea of a royal Messiah.

This vast, national sadness offered the prophets the opportunity to face up to the problem of suffering and its relationship to covenant and redemption. Their long thoughts came to a peak in the now famous "servant poems" as found in chapters 42, 49, 50, 52, and 53 of Isaiah. No longer does a triumphant, royal messianic king hold the center of the stage. Now, it is the servant of Yahweh, called by the Spirit, entrusted with the vocation to bring justice to the nations, who solves the riddle of suffering by giving it value in the form of salvation.

Salvation is accomplished through the voluntary acceptance of suffering by the anointed servant of the Lord: "Surely he has borne our griefs and carried our sorrows; yet we esteemed him stricken, smitten by God, and afflicted. But he was wounded for our transgressions, he was bruised for our iniquities; upon him was the chastisement that made us whole, and with his stripes we are healed" (Isaiah 53:4-5).

New Testament writers were quick to employ the theme of the servant as a principal messianic title for Jesus, especially in the light of His agony and crucifixion. The earliest preaching of the apostolic Church often used the servant theme (see Acts 8:30-35). Saint Peter included the idea in his letters: "He himself bore our sins in his body on the tree, that we might die to sin and live to righteousness. By his wounds you have been healed" (1 Peter 2:24).

THE SON OF MAN

Toward the end of the Old Testament period a third theme appears, that of the man from heaven, or the "Son of Man," as found in the prophecy of Daniel. In Daniel's seventh chapter, he relates a nightmarish dream in which stormy winds bring forth four monsters from a black lake. These monsters gain control of the earth and tyrannize its peoples. What this really means is that the first creation went awry and men did not fulfill their destiny as true images of God serving mankind out of love and concern.

The dream continues with a white-bearded, fiery-eyed judge, called the "Ancient of Days," setting up a throne of judgment against sinful mankind. He takes away from sinful nations the control of the earth. At that moment, a glorious sky figure, called the "Son of Man," journeys across the heavens, his face totally fixed on the Ancient of Days. In the Garden of Eden, the old Adam had turned his face away from the Lord and had hid himself from His gaze. Daniel sees this new heavenly Adam as a messianic figure. To this glorious sky figure the Ancient of Days gives dominion over the earth.

KING, SUFFERING SERVANT, SON OF MAN

It is not hard to see how these three ideas about the Messiah (king, suffering servant, Son of Man) found their way into the gospel accounts. Popular piety was naturally interested in the royal Messiah, because of the stirring memories of the glories of King David and the humiliation of a subjected people. The common people plainly wanted a political liberator. But those who lived on a deeper level of faith realized that a spiritual salvation was also required. Thus, they were sympathetic to the religious teaching about the Messiah seen as a suffering servant.

Jesus was not unwilling to be identified with the Davidic and servant titles. But He is often best remembered for taking as His own the title of Son of Man. In this way, He was showing that His messianic destiny included the founding of a new mankind, a new creation wherein He would take charge of the earth. He would become the Lord of the universe and would share this rule of the earth with the Church that He intended to found. In this light, the Church becomes a messianic community bent on ordering the earth to the glory of God and the love of man.

This rich prophetic vision of the Messiah as a royal king, a suffering servant, and the new Adam helps us in our understanding of Jesus.

HE SAW THE GLORY OF THE LORD
The Prophet Isaiah

The story of the prophets is, among other things, a litany of condemnation of sin. Samuel rapped the knuckles of the priest, Heli, whose sons leered at young female worshipers and cheated the simple peasants who brought gifts to the Lord. Nathan pointed an accusing finger at King David for his terrible injustice to Uriah: David sent Uriah to his death in battle and then married his wife. Elijah fumed with anger against the atrocities and idolatries of King Ahab and Queen Jezebel.

Isaiah is equally direct in accusing the people of their basic sinfulness. The irony is that he comes to this insight as a result of an encounter with the glory of God, described in the memory of his vision which is preserved in the sixth chapter of the book of Isaiah.

ISAIAH'S VISION

In the year that King Uzziah died, the young aristocrat, Isaiah, went to the temple for some elaborate liturgical ceremony. Because of his privileged position in society, he was shown to one of the front seats. There he sat amid a heady atmosphere provided by clouds of sweet incense, rhythmic chant, the stately paces of liturgical movement, and the rich, colorful attire of the participants. The backdrop for the rite was the temple building. Inside it was the Holy of Holies wherein reposed the ark of the covenant. Resting on the ark were the angelic seraphim, upon whose wings would rest the cloud-glory of God's presence.

As Isaiah is caught up in this atmosphere, the Lord God lifts him up to the dimensions of vision. While Isaiah peers into the thick darkness of the room enclosing the Holy of Holies, the liturgy surrounding him seems to give way to a vision of a liturgical celebration in heaven.

Isaiah sees the Lord "sitting upon a throne, high and lifted up." His robe seems to fill the temple. This description means that the awesome presence of God penetrates the entire place. The servants at God's throne are seraphim—fire angels, associated with the glory of the Lord. Each angel has six wings and uses two wings to cover his face. This masking symbolizes the mystery of God, much the same as a masked face holds mystery for us, and sometimes terror. The angels appear to be saying: no one may look upon the face of God and live. As he looks upon the vision, Isaiah hears the chant about God's holiness and glory, as, in the New Testament, the shepherds one day hear angels on the hillside of Bethlehem sing about the glory of Jesus.

ISAIAH EXPERIENCES THE HOLINESS AND GLORY OF GOD

The song about God's holiness is a way of emphasizing His opposition to sin. A German writer, Rudolph Otto, says that holiness is an experience of fear and fascination on our part. Moses approaches the holy ground of Mount Horeb before the burning bush, *fascinated* by this marvel, yet *fearfully* taking off his shoes and bowing to the earth at a respectful distance from the bush. Peter, James, and John react in a similar fashion before the burning glory of Christ at His transfiguration (*see* page 300).

Next, in the biblical account of Isaiah's vision, "the foundations

THE PROPHET ISAIAH, *during a ceremony in the temple, had a vision: he saw the glory of the Lord*

of the threshold shook" (Isaiah 6:4). As thunder and lightning and the roar of the sea made primitive man understand the might of God, so here the trembling of the temple foundations brings Isaiah to know the Almighty. After this, the vision blacks out in smoke. Isaiah stands dazed and alone. He gradually becomes aware of himself in contrast to what he has seen. In his weak and sinful condition, he has confronted the matchless holiness and glory of god.

Isaiah looks into his own heart and makes a serious examination of conscience. This scrutiny impels him to utter the anguished admission: "Woe is me! For I am lost; for I am a man of unclean lips." He goes on to assure us of the real reason why he can make this judgment of himself: "For my eyes have seen the King, the Lord of hosts!" Unclean lips is an expression of human selfishness, a way of speaking about one's sinfulness.

A BURNING COAL CLEANSES THE LIPS OF THE PROPHET

Now the cloud disappears, and the vision returns. One of the fire angels (a seraph) takes a hot coal from the altar of incense, and presses it against the unclean lips of the prophet, and recites what is reminiscent of a sacramental formula: "Behold, this has touched your lips; your guilt is taken away and your sin forgiven." The purifying coal of fire is a symbol of God saving men through His transforming power.

And now God speaks: "Whom shall I send, and who will go for us?" The Lord has a mission for the prophet. His words to Isaiah are framed in such a way that the prophet remains free to accept or reject the commission. The cleansed Isaiah, possessing a new heart forged by the divine courage, looks into the face of God and says: "Here am I! Send me."

Notice the rhythm of the movement in this vision. God advances first upon the prophet, breaking into his prayerful mood at a liturgical function. The actions of Isaiah are a response resulting

ISAIAH'S VISION: *"the foundations of the threshold shook, and the temple was filled with smoke"*

from his awareness of the divine initiative. God speaks to him with a vision of His unapproachable glory and holiness. Isaiah responds with his confession that he is a sinful man. God speaks to the prophet again, this time with the purifying fire of the seraph, and a call to apostolic mission in this world. Isaiah makes the total response of obedience and love.

CHRIST CLEANSES US IN THE SACRAMENT OF PENANCE

This account of the call of Isaiah suggests God's approach to sinful men today. When God looks upon a sinful man, He approaches him in some mysterious way, awakening in him a sense of the divine purity and his contrasting sinfulness. Christ, the new pillar of fire, the new fire angel, descends upon the sinner with the glowing coal of the sacrament of penance, removing all guilt and sin. With this comes the immediate call to reaffirm the decision to really live as a Christian.

Isaiah, then, saw the glory of God. It was a shattering experience, making him radically reconsider the meaning of his own life, and undertake a new mission. He knew that this would not be easy. God's demand was strong: "Make the heart of this people fat, and their ears heavy, and shut their eyes; lest they see with their eyes, and hear with their ears, and understand with their hearts, and turn and be healed."

Faced with this difficult task, the prophet understandably and hopefully asks: "How long, O Lord?" And God replied: "Until cities lie waste without inhabitant . . . and the forsaken places are many in the midst of the land." This is not exactly the most comforting sort of future. Isaiah can anticipate a career that will meet with constant frustration and rejection because the people are spiritually blind and deaf. Hence the judgment will bring their lands to waste.

A FEW HEAR GOD'S WORDS AND REMAIN FAITHFUL

The encouraging part of God's message is that a remnant of people will remain. Isaiah can count on a small group who will indeed understand his message and remain faithful. They, too, will experience the fires of purification: "And though a tenth remain in it, it will be burned again, like a terebinth or an oak, whose stump remains standing when it is felled. The holy seed [remnant] is its stump" (see Isaiah chapter 6).

Historically, the nation went up in flames at the time of the Babylonian invasion. The holy remnant was the group of Israelites that were taken into Babylonian exile where they knew the purification of seventy years (*see* page 132). They preserved the stirring memory of Isaiah, his vision of glory, his own painful purification, and his tireless efforts to summon the nation to penance and to encourage the faithful few. Read all of Isaiah, chapter six, to get the flavor of the prophet's vision, purification, and mission.

THE LOSS OF A TRUE SENSE OF SIN

The Preaching of the Prophet Jeremiah

History is full of men who have failed to take personal responsibility. In recent years newspapers have been filled
with stories and editorials dealing with the breakdown of personal
responsibility in our times. There are those who have witnessed
the rape of young girls and the murder of old men, and have not
had the decency or moral strength to call for police help or to use
their own abilities to defend the weak. This problem of accepting
or avoiding personal responsibility is a very old one, and one that
each generation of men must accept and face.

MAN FOUND SECURITY IN GROUP STRENGTH

In biblical times, people went through a twofold phase before
the issue of personal responsibility was adequately faced. During
the patriarchal and tribal confederacy periods, group or communal
responsibility was stressed. The individual person found his
strength and identity in the collective power of the tribe. His
mentality was always in terms of the group, whether in such
matters as finding a new water hole or in fighting off a hostile
tribe or in seeking revenge for the slaughter of one of his own
tribe.

In such an atmosphere, it was only natural that the responsibility for a moral collapse would be considered communal. After all, punishment for sins was experienced in that way. For example, the army of Joshua experienced a puzzling defeat at the gates of Ai just after it had won a resounding victory at Jericho. The reason for the defeat was that one member of Joshua's army had sinned by stealing silver and gold from Jericho and had buried the treasure in the ground as a selfish hoard for himself. Nevertheless, the entire army (seen as the community) was held responsible for the crime, and was therefore defeated (punished). The punishment of the individual criminal, Achan, was severe: he was stoned to death.

SENSE OF SIN LOST: NO ONE FELT RESPONSIBLE

The difficulty that arises with the group idea of responsibility is that sin can soon lose its personal aspect. If everybody sins, then it begins to seem as if nobody sins. Centuries of the group approach to morality withers away the sense of sin. And this fact becomes all the more evident as the tribal form of society simultaneously disappears. This is what had happened in Israel by the time of the prophet Jeremiah.

The fierce blood and social connections of Israel's tribal days had yielded to the fragmented life of the monarchy in which the aristocrats had formed their own social set, prophetic communities had become groups apart, and the poor had been dispersed into villages that soon forgot the fierce tribal loyalties of former days. With the disappearance of the strict tribal form, what remained of the idea of group morality made less sense to the Israelites.

Within the nation itself, it seemed that the sense of sin had been nearly lost. The chosen people had retained a communal sense of responsibility while their community had substantially disappeared. But along the way, the idea of communal morality had been dropped. The idea of sin had been changed into some sort of impersonal *it* for which no one felt responsibility, either personal or communal. At this point, it is useful to study the temple sermon of Jeremiah in the book of Jeremiah, chapter seven.

In his blistering sermon on the false use of the temple, Jeremiah showed that just as the Israelites had a false notion of how God's blessings came to them, they had also a false notion of sin. He found them chattering the formula, "temple of the Lord," as though it were a magic chant which could charm away their sins and win blessings.

SIN IS A PERSONAL REFUSAL TO LOVE AND OBEY GOD

The temple was not supposed to be a mere *thing*. It was intended to be holy ground, the sacred space where man could enter into dialogue with God. And if the temple became an "it" because God was no longer seen as a "Thou" – a partner in a very personal relationship – then sin became no more than the violation of a command, and neither a communal nor a personal refusal to love and obey God.

Once God is depersonalized – seen as a "thing" – then sin, too, becomes a matter of offense against an "it." Instead of "Thou" and "Him," we now have an "it." And when this happens, we start to measure our lives against an abstract command, rather than against the love offered us by our Father who wants to save us.

Jeremiah stood by the crowded temple gate and raised his voice against the smug throngs gaily tossing off their sins by smirkingly and thoughtlessly muttering canned prayers. Jeremiah warned the people: "Do not trust in these deceptive words" (Jeremiah 7:4). He drew their attention to the real problem – *the loss of genuine contact with God*. He accused them of stealing, murdering, cheating, lying, and fornicating and then, hypocritically, rushing off to the temple with a twinge of conscience, to say they were delivered – and then continue these evil acts.

Jeremiah uttered words that later would be adapted by Jesus:

THE PROPHET JEREMIAH *summoned Baruch, the son of Neriah,*
"and Baruch wrote upon a scroll at the dictation of Jeremiah
all the words of the Lord which He had spoken to him" (Jere-
miah 36:4)

"Has this house, which is called by my name, become a den of robbers in your eyes?" (Jeremiah 7:11). Jeremiah reminded the people how God had destroyed the shrine at Shilo in the northern kingdom, where He had also established His name. God had wiped out that shrine because the people had made it a mere thing of magic. Jeremiah assured them that God is perfectly willing to repeat this performance.

PERSONAL RESPONSIBILITY BEFORE A PERSONAL GOD

Jeremiah told them that they were a foolish people who rushed about baking bread and stamping the dough with the image of the pagan queen of the heavens. They, the holy people of God, blissfully ignored the primary address of God: "Obey my voice, and I will be your God, and you shall be my people; and walk in all the way that I command you, that it may be well with you" (Jeremiah 7:23).

Fearlessly, Jeremiah pronounced doom for those who disregarded genuine contact with God and committed themselves to a purely external and materialistic religion. He warned them that such sinners would "be food for the birds of the air, and none will frighten them away." The sound of mirth and the voice of gladness would disappear from the streets. The gay shouts of bridal processions would be heard no more, for the city would become a desolation. Bones of the dead would be taken from the grave and spread before the sun and moon which they loved and served, consulted and worshiped. These bones would be left as dung upon the face of the earth.

Jeremiah has placed before our eyes a scene from a religion of superstition rooted in the chill world of stones and charm formulas, a religion in which God is a thing and not a person. He has sketched for us the image of those who have lost their sense of a personal God. He has made a direct attack on the consciences of his listeners. By appealing to each one to turn to God as a "thou,"

Jeremiah has, at the same time, quickened the conscience of the individual and forced him to accept responsibility for his moral life.

SENSE OF SIN LOST TODAY

Men of today have also lost the sense of sin. Irreligious people simply say there is no sin. Religious people come to the same conclusion by hedging sin within some abstract category, absolving themselves from it by the uttering of some safe formula that charms away the guilt and produces the illusion of absolution. That is why Christians can stand by when others are being beaten and attacked, because for them sin has lost its personal meaning, and individual responsibility is meaningless.

Listen to the prayer of Jeremiah in chapter 17:

> "Heal me, O Lord, and I shall be healed;
>   save me, and I shall be saved;
>   for you are my praise. . . .
> Be not a terror to me;
>   you are my refuge in the day of evil"
>   (Jeremiah 17:14–17).

WORSHIP THAT HAS REVERENCE FOR THE HOLINESS OF GOD
The Teaching of the Prophet Ezekiel

Space buffs might enjoy the flying saucer atmosphere of the opening chapter of the book of Ezekiel. The prophet Ezekiel is seated along the banks of the River Chebar in ancient Babylon, having followed the Hebrew community into exile (*see* page 132). The heavens open, the earthly scene fades, and the prophet sees whirling wheels, four-faced men, crystal skies, and a sapphire throne in a vision. This experience serves as the background of Ezekiel's call to be a prophet.

THE BOOK OF EZEKIEL

It is comparatively easy to see the outline of his book. After the story telling of his call to be a prophet, which occupies the first three chapters, there follows the series of sermons which Ezekiel delivered in Jerusalem. In these, he criticized the people for their evil ways and fortold their doom. This section is followed by angry warnings against the heathen nations, and the Israelites who held beliefs similar to those of the Gentiles. The third section of the book is a diary of Ezekiel's sermons to the Jews now in exile. He changes from harsh condemnation to inspirational talks which attempt to strengthen their hopes.

The last part of the book (chapters 40 to 48) is the prophet's record of what the new temple should be like after the group returns from exile. Ezekiel not only details temple construction, but also outlines a sort of religious constitution for the community after the exile.

A PLAN OF RELIGIOUS LIVING

The language used by Ezekiel to describe the new temple and form of religion suggests that he is having a vision. But his purpose is to give the future congregations a plan of religious living that will ward off the anger of God, which has cast the present community into exile.

These closing chapters of the book of Ezekiel form the most original and influential part of the prophet's work. He gives a remarkably complete outline of the ritual and church structures which should be adopted by the new community. Here he was, a Jew living in exile with a people who, as an alien minority, had neither political power nor rights nor any temple where they could sacrifice. This absence of ceremonial religion made it seem all the more important that they prepare for the restoration of divinely revealed worship.

Ezekiel had an amazing knowledge of Solomon's temple and its ritual practice. Much of this was used in his new plan. He leaves practically nothing out: the description of the temple courts, the sacristies for the clergy, the exact measurements of the structure, the ritual for the dedication of the altar, the plan for the temple kitchens. He ends with a vision of the glory of God taking up a permanent abode in the new temple after having abandoned the old temple of Solomon.

HE CALLED FOR WORSHIP EMPHASIZING GOD'S HOLINESS

Before the exile, Ezekiel had emphasized the justice and mercy of God and the ethical demands made of a pious Jew. Now, as he looks ahead to the congregation of the future, he underlines the

EZEKIEL, *the prophet of the exile, taught his people that each person is responsible before God, and that true religion is not an external show but an inner strength*

holiness of God and the methods of preserving a reverence for this holiness: "Her priests have done violence to my law and have profaned my holy things; they have made no distinction between the holy and the common . . . they have disregarded my sabbaths, so that I am profaned among them" (Ezekiel 22:26).

He felt, quite rightly, that the the lack of reverence for God's holy name and holy things was one of the capital sins of Israel. "But I had concern for my holy name which the house of Israel caused to be profaned. . . . You have despised my holy things, and profaned my sabbaths" (Ezekiel 36:21; 22:8). Ezekiel's new program was designed to prevent future national disaster by forestalling any new disregard for the sacredness of God.

The prophet's principal solution to the problem of preserving a reverence for the holiness of God was to isolate the sacred from the profane. His plan was something like the precautions taken by a modern hospital staff to insure the purity of an operating room. Ezekiel's ground plan for the temple insured the isolation. His rules for worship were a sort of sterilization process. The walls would keep out the profane.

By emphasizing the holiness of the temple, Ezekiel excluded the invasion of the profane. Here God would have His throne. By contrast, the old temple was too careless about contact with the profane. The royal palace was on the temple grounds, as were the kings' tombs. Uncircumcised foreigners were used as janitors, and unlawful practices had been introduced within the temple precincts.

Ezekiel called for moving the new temple a mile south of the old one. He blocked off a holy zone that included the central space for the temple, land for the temple clergy, and a residential area for the Levites. The city should be situated south of the temple.

TEMPLE PRACTICES DRASTICALLY CHANGED

The building already surrounded by the domain of the clergy would have two walled courtyards instead of Solomon's one. The

THE PROPHET EZEKIEL'S *book was so influential on the religious life of Israel, he has often been called "the father of Judaism"*

walls were intended to separate the holy from the common. The sanctuary was in the inner court. Laymen would worship in the outer court, and would not take part in the sacrificial ceremonies. In actual fact, however, the laymen refused to give up their ancient right to offer their own sacrifices in the inner court.

Ezekiel did succeed in getting rid of the alien janitors. The Levites assumed these menial duties. The book of Deuteronomy equates the Levites with the priests. But from the time of Ezekiel, the Levites became only assistants to the priests. The prophet's attention to the most minute details of temple furnishing and ritual showed his consuming desire to keep the holy place from any profanation. He composed rules about such things as the offering of animals and vegetables, the materials and tailoring of the priestly vestments, the opening and closing of gates. This reverence for the holy was intended to remove God's anger.

Ezekiel was aware that human error and mistake must be dealt with. Hence, he prescribed purification rituals. His attention was focused totally on public worship, because his concern was to preserve a friendly relationship between God and the whole nation. He had little interest in private sacrifice. He concentrated on a worship that paid tribute to the divine and purified transgressions, unwitting or otherwise. Therefore, he introduced a gloomy solemnity to religious practice which suppressed the spontaneous gladness of earlier worship.

THE FATHER OF JUDAISM

So influential was Ezekiel's book on the religious life of Israel that he has been called by some the "father of Judaism." From him, the Jews inherited a personal sense of the need for repentance, an awesome sense of reverence for God, and an abiding hatred of idolatry. His liturgical reform was radical and lasting. It had the weakness of being overorganized, leaving little room for the spontaneous. But the reform did put fiber into the national religion.

His hopes eventually led to ritual legalism, but Ezekiel's legacy of the need to reverence the holy did not die. He was a grouchy, sometimes almost fanatical prophet, but one whose basic wisdom instilled a sense of responsibility into a perpetually thoughtless people. Today, we would not enjoy his rigidity, but we can celebrate his "legacy of the holy" as we ourselves engage in liturgical reform.

A TEENAGE HERO
The Prophet Daniel

Teenagers have been accused of many things, but rarely have they been called prophets. The Bible, however, tells the story of a prophet who was a teenager. His prophecies and his life story are as unusual as the fact of his youth. His name was Daniel, which means "God has judged."

SIX STORIES AND FOUR VISIONS

The book of Daniel is made up of six colorful stories and four visions. It borrows images from natural disasters. The author of the book of Daniel lived under the Greek persecution of Antiochus the Terrible, from 167 to 164 B.C. He was sensitive to the national despair brought on by this persecution, and so told six legendlike tales that survived the Babylonian experience years before (*see* page 132). He used these stories as inspirational narratives to hearten the faithful of his time. Then he used the four visions of Daniel as ways of interpreting the meaning of the present crisis and establishing hope in the ultimate victory of the saints of God.

DANIEL AND HIS FRIENDS BROUGHT
INTO THE SERVICE OF THE KING

The first story about Daniel is placed against the background of the Babylonian captivity and the slave policies of the king. The monarch of Babylon had decided that the cream of the conquered youth should be brought into the service of the king. "Then the king commanded Ashpenaz, his chief eunuch, to bring . . . youths without blemish, handsome and skillful in all wisdom . . . to serve in the king's palace" (Daniel 1:3-4).

Attention is drawn to the person of Daniel and his three friends. Negro spirituals have immortalized their three names: Shadrach, Meshach, and Abednego. Their first problem was one of diet. The rules called for them to become accustomed to Babylonian menus. But, unfortunately, this conflicted with the dietary rules of the Hebrews. To conform meant they would be unfaithful to their religion. "But Daniel resolved that he would not defile himself with the king's rich food" (Daniel 1:8).

DANIEL STANDS UP FOR HIS BELIEFS

Daniel was only a teenager, but he was not afraid to stand up for his beliefs, even against so imposing a figure as the king of Babylon. Daniel proposed a compromise. He insisted that he and his friends be put on a vegetarian diet, promising that they would be as healthy as the others after a ten-day period. The gentle man in charge agreed, and was pleasantly surprised to find that at the end of ten days, "they were better in appearance and fatter in flesh than all the youths who ate the king's rich food" (Daniel 1:15).

Then Daniel and his friends were presented to the king and found great favor with him. Daniel emerged as a wise man, even though he was still a youth. Each of the stories that follows this account illustrates in different ways Daniel's wisdom. He had become a wise man because, on the one hand, he did not fear the

DANIEL *was thrown into the lions' den and told "your God will have to save you." Next day, he was released "and found to be unhurt because he had trusted in his God"* (Daniel 6:23)

might of kings, and on the other, he stood by his conviction that obedience to his God was all important.

DANIEL INTERPRETED DREAMS

By his obedience to the Lord, Daniel began to share in the creative power and wisdom of the Lord. One biblical way of illustrating this was by showing his ability to interpret dreams. The second story, then, is about a dream. The king saw a giant statue which had feet of clay. A small stone was enough to topple the image. When the king awoke, he did not remember what the dream was about, let alone understand its meaning. He asked his court advisers to help him out, but they were helpless.

Then Daniel appeared with the details of the dream and its meaning. The statue was made of various metals: these referred to the different empires which had ruled the world. The feet of clay meant that all of these empires were ultimately destined to fall. The small stone which rolled against the monstrous image and overcame it represented the small community who were faithful to God and were seeking justice. This stone eventually rose until it became a mountain that touched the heavens. "But the stone that struck the image became a great mountain" (Daniel 2:35).

This image of the small rock that became a mountain rising up to God and filling the earth may offer us some insight into the account in which Christ addresses Himself to Peter the "rock," telling Peter that upon this small rock will be built the Church. And this Church will be a mountain rising to heaven.

THE DEN OF LIONS

The other stories about the wise and courageous young Daniel repeat the themes of his insight and religious dedication. His three friends were thrown into a fiery furnace, but were saved by the protective cloak of their faith. Daniel himself was hurled into a den of growling and hungry lions, but his faith subdued the

DANIEL *was cast into the lions' den, yet remained unharmed. God protected him,
Daniel said, "since in His sight I am blame-
less"*

angry beasts, creating a scene like the garden of paradise in which
Daniel was a new Adam controlling the animal world.

VISION OF THE FOUR BEASTS

Among the four visions in the book of Daniel, the one in chapter
seven deserves our attention. Daniel had a nightmare in which he
heard the blast of the four winds of the world beating over the
black waters of a vast lake. He saw a lion, a bear, and a leopard
and finally a beast beyond description. "After this I saw in the
night visions, and behold, a fourth beast, terrible and dreadful
and exceedingly strong; and it had great iron teeth; it devoured
and broke in pieces, and stamped the residue with its feet."
(Daniel 7:7).

The black lake represented the chaos that existed before creation. The four winds were symbolic of the creative breath of God
that brought forth the first mankind. The four beasts represented

the different generations of the old mankind who were given dominion over the earth. Picturing them as beasts with cruel intent taught that the first mankind did not really become the image of God and so did not deserve to inherit and rule the earth (*see* page 23).

The dream next introduced a scene of light. An old man called "the Ancient of Days" ascended a throne of judgment: "the court sat in judgment, and the books were opened" (Daniel 7:10). The Ancient of Days declared that the dominion of the earth would now be taken away from the four beasts. Then he turned and saw the "son of man" coming toward him across the heavens. The expression "son of man" here seems to mean the new mankind which turns its face to the Creator and is, therefore, worthy to become the new heirs of the kingdom. "And to him was given dominion and glory. . . . The saints of the Most High shall receive the kingdom . . . forever and ever" (Daniel 7:14, 18).

JESUS CALLED HIMSELF THE SON OF MAN

The purpose of this vision was to encourage the Jews living under the persecution of Antiochus the Terrible. Beastlike tyrants like Antiochus would eventually be overcome by the power of God, as one day He would establish a new age that would be characterized by a faithful and obedient mankind.

In the Gospels, we can note that Jesus was very fond of referring to Himself as the "Son of Man," the title from the book of Daniel. Jesus is the new Adam to whom has been given the lordship of the world, and who shares this loving dominion with the saints of the most high, namely, the Church. The Church is a dominion of love and service that is truly creative.

The prophetic spirit of Daniel lives in many teenagers today who have developed a sense of concern for people who are unjustly treated in our world. Jesus noted that at times it is from the young that wisdom comes.

A FARMER URGES SOCIAL REFORM
The Prophet Amos

The image that religious leaders often leave is that of highly refined and cultured men. It is, then, refreshing to come to the story of Amos, who was unashamedly a mountaineer, and had no intention of hiding his rustic ways as farmer and shepherd. He lived in 750 B.C., in Tekoa, a mountain village in the wilderness of Judah.

Amos' call to prophecy came while he was watching his sheep. God summoned him to go from town to town in the northern kingdom of Israel. Perhaps his most famous phrase is the expression he hurled at the women's club in Samaria where he called these ladies of high fashion, "cows of Bashan" (*see* Amos 4:1–3).

AMOS CRITICIZED LUXURIOUS LIVING

Like many of the prophets, Amos criticized luxurious living. He preached at the shrine cities such as Gilgal. His career was suddenly brought to a halt by Amaziah, the president of the royal sanctuary at Bethel. Amaziah accused Amos of heresy, a charge that was mixed with accusations of treason against King Jeroboam II. He succeeded in suddenly ending the prophetic activity of Amos after a few brief months. "O seer, go, flee away to the land of Judah, and eat bread there, and prophesy there; but never again prophesy at Bethel, for it is the king's sanctuary, and it is a temple of the kingdom" (Amos 7:12–13).

Amos retired gracefully, but with a biting rejoinder to the hypocritical Amaziah:

"Your wife shall be a harlot in the city, and your sons and your daughters shall fall by the sword, and your land shall be parceled out by line; you yourself shall die in an unclean land" (Amos 7:17).

It is no simple matter to preach repentance to a prosperous people. Amos' prophecies coincided with the last burst of luxurious living Israel knew before her downfall. Israel had a boom economy because of several successful wars and, as a result, the merchant princes were living high. In the golden glow of this prosperity, the people could scarcely believe that the doom perceived by Amos could really happen. It is a tribute to Amos' genius that he really could sense the true threat presented by Assyria, even though at that time this threat was but a cloud on the horizon, no larger than a man's hand.

GOD IS LORD OF ALL NATIONS

Amos was the first of the great reforming prophets. He was also the first to preach that God was the Lord of all nations, not just the Lord of Israel. In the general thinking of the time, each nation had its own God. Israel thought no differently. Yahweh was her God, greater indeed than all gods, but not the only god. But Amos spoke of Yahweh as Lord of every nation. He spoke of the Lord giving land to other nations besides Israel. It is true that God had put a special amount of attention on Israel, but only because He wanted a higher standard for her. "You only have I known of all the families of the earth; therefore, I will punish you for all your iniquities" (Amos 3:2).

It is easy to see how Amos seemed like a real heretic: his message was so new; none of the other prophets had spoken this way.

THE PROPHET AMOS *preached against dishonesty: "Hear this,*
you who trample upon the needy and bring the poor of the land
to an end . . . and deal deceitfully with false balances . . ."
(Amos 8:4–5)

In fact, Amos did not want to be identified with the other prophets. "I am a herdsman, and a dresser of sycamore trees." But he also insisted that he truly represented the true message of the Lord: "The Lord took me from following the flock, and the Lord said to me, 'Go, prophesy to my people Israel'" (Amos 7:14–15).

He was not out to found a new religion, but to establish the old one in spirit and truth. He shifted the emphasis from external forms to the purification of the people's conscience. He insisted that Yahweh, the God of all nations, would not die with the fall of Israel. In fact, it is precisely this God who would annihilate Israel.

ISRAEL IGNORED THE POOR AND PRACTICED FALSE PIETY

As a genuine social reformer, Amos was horrified by the departure of Israel from even the simplest standards of decency that any civilized nation would uphold. He saw dishonesty. "Hear this, you who trample upon the needy, and bring the poor of the land to an end, saying 'When will the new moon be over that we may sell grain? And the sabbath . . . that we may make the ephah [bushel] small . . . and deal deceitfully with false balances. . . ?'" (Amos 8:4–5). He noticed the people's ruthlessness. In the face of such poverty, he was shocked by the luxury of the palaces and mansions of the rich. "Woe to those who lie upon beds of ivory . . . and eat lambs from the flock . . . who sing idle songs to the sound of the harp . . . and anoint themselves with the finest oils, but are not grieved over the ruin of Joseph!" (Amos 6:4–6).

In condemning such self-indulgence, he used strong language. "I abhor the pride of Jacob, and hate his strongholds; and I will deliver up the city and all that is in it" (Amos 6:8). The irony of it all was that the people of Israel not only forgot the plight of the poor, but cushioned their consciences by performing all the tried and true religious ceremonies that honored their God. In following the traditional acts of religious piety, they felt that that was

THE PROPHET AMOS *preached against the swindlers and exploiters "who trample on the needy and try to suppress the poor people of the country"*

all God needed to keep from being angry or threatening them. They used the very liturgy itself as a wall to insulate themselves from any concern for the poor.

Even degrading aspects of their piety did not shame them. Amos noted that fathers and sons sinned with the same woman, even in the temple area, and got drunk there on wine purchased with money from unfair fines. It is understandable, then, that Amos had such hard words for a liturgy among such an immoral people. "I hate, I despise your feasts, and I take no delight in your solemn assemblies. Even though you offer me your burnt offerings . . . I will not accept them" (Amos 5:21).

Amos was not opposed to liturgy in itself, but to a worship performed by such an immoral people. God will not tolerate a liturgy divorced from a proper spirit. Splendid sacrifices, huge feast-day crowds, and loud music are not a substitute for clean lives. Some have accused Amos of being opposed to liturgy itself, but this is not true. His eye was on the heart, not the ceremony. Amos insisted on the need for social justice along with liturgy.

REAL MEANING OF LITURGY IS SEEN IN SOCIAL JUSTICE, RIGHT LIVING

The brief ministry of Amos gave the world one of the first documents of social protest. He had the courage to be a reformer, and the genius to see through the trappings of power and wealth to the rot that lay beneath. He showed that real liturgical relevance is not a matter of fresh ceremonies, but is rooted in right living and compassion for the poor and unjustly treated. Rough hewn as he was, Amos loved Israel. That love can be seen in this quiet lament: "Fallen, no more to rise, is the virgin Israel; forsaken on her land, with none to raise her up" (Amos 5:2). He scourged Israel because he loved her, and wept over her because she loved neither God nor man.

GOD'S MARVELOUS LOYALTY TO HIS PLEDGE
The Prophet Hosea

It is common enough for an adulterous woman to be one of the central figures in a modern novel. But when this is true of a biblical book, we can understandably be surprised. Yet this is precisely what happens in the book of Hosea, the prophet. Gomer, the prophet's wife, was unfaithful to him.

THE MAIN ISSUE IS ISRAEL'S FIDELITY TO GOD

It is true that there is some confusion about this. Chapters one and three have two different stories about what God really asked Hosea to do. The first chapter seems to indicate that he should marry a woman who would become an adulteress. The third chapter, on the other hand, seems to say that Hosea should marry a woman who is already guilty of fornication. While most critics will argue over whether chapter one or three is the true story, they all admit that the main issue is not really Hosea's domestic problems, but Israel's fidelity to God. At most, the faithless Gomer is an image of faithless Israel.

THE IMPORTANCE OF A PERSON'S NAME

The opening chapter of the book of Hosea tells of Hosea's marriage to Gomer and the three children that she bore him. Great attention is paid to the names given the children, especially to their symbolism. At first sight this can seem unimportant to us, because we more than likely share Shakespeare's thought: "What's in a name? . . . a rose by any other name would smell as sweet." But for biblical people, a name was very important. It signified the power or office of a person.

Names deal with a person's destiny. For example, Abram became Abraham, for he was to be the father of all nations. Simon became Peter, for he would be the rock upon which Christ's Church would be built. And even in our own society, names can be more important than we might at first imagine. Salesmen know that their customers like to be known by name. Politicians have long known the same thing is valuable in vote getting. The legendary Jim Farley, Franklin Roosevelt's campaign manager, is said to have known fifty thousand people by name.

Hosea and Gomer gave their children symbolic names. They named their first son, Jezreel, which was the name of one of the royal residences. This residence had become a scene of horror where the king, Jehu, massacred the decendants of Omri, a former king. The name of Hosea's son was a reminder to King Jehu that God intended to punish him for this crime.

ISRAEL, LIKE GOMER, IS UNFAITHFUL

Then they had a daughter whom they named "Not Pitied." This was a way of telling Israel, the northern kingdom, that her days were numbered because of her infidelity. Their third child was another boy, whom they called, "Not My People." God's gift of election would now pass to the southern kingdom of Judah alone. Each child represented the increasing alienation of Israel from God, ending in total rejection.

The second chapter shifts from Hosea's domestic situation to a conversation between God and His faithless wife, Israel. Here we have a fascinating description of how God tries tirelessly to keep Israel united to Him. At the beginning of the chapter, God

HOSEA'S *wife, Gomer, was unfaithful to him, but he loved her and forgave her. In like manner, Israel was unfaithful to God, but He continues to love His people*

assumes the attitude of a slighted lover. Then, by repeated attempts at correcting His beloved, He seeks to win her back. His first punishment is to treat her like a shameless woman, according to the customs of the time.

He will then rob the land of all fertility and prosperity. "Therefore, I will take back my grain . . . and my wine. . . . And I will lay waste her vines and her fig trees. . . . I will make them a forest and the beasts of the field shall devour them."

RETURN TO THE INNOCENCE OF THE DAYS IN THE DESERT

Happily, these corrective tests work, for, having removed the demoralizing luxury of Israel, God brings her into a desert where she can know Him again. "Therefore, behold, I will allure her, and bring her into the wilderness, and speak tenderly to her. . . . And there she shall answer as in the days of her youth" (Hosea 2:14–15). The real clue in this passage is the word "desert." As the centuries passed, the memory of Israel's days in the desert during the time of the exodus (*see* page 67) was idealized. If distance lends enchantment to the view, then this is a fine example. The passage of time tended to glamorize the innocence and childlikeness of that early desert community. It is perfectly human to gloss over the harsh features of the distant past and endow it with a dreamlike quality.

After all, Israel's wanderings in the desert was a time when Israel knew no other God but Yahweh. That was when she really knew how to be His bride. Other prophets would be equally strong in picking up the desert theme as a lever for promoting reform among the Israelites. In other words, the prophets urged Israel to return to the ideals found in the origin of the race. It is something like telling present Notre Dame football players to remember former greats like Knute Rockne and George Gipp. This has an inspirational value as well as a current lesson for the hearers.

Thus, God, having removed the material prosperity of Israel,

THE PROPHET HOSEA *told his people that despite their unfaithfulness God continues to honor the covenant He made with them*

put her in a sort of desert where she could think about turning to Him again in love. When she renewed her commitment to Him, He would give her back the vineyards, send rain from the sky and harvests from the earth. Wild animals would not harm her, nor would enemy nations wage war against her. "And I will betroth you to me for ever . . . in justice, in steadfast love, and in mercy" (Hosea 2:19).

GOD REMAINS FAITHFUL TO HIS PEOPLE

The principal message of the whole book is brought out in this line: "I will betroth you to me in faithfulness" (Hosea 2:20). The translation of the Jerusalem Bible is worth quoting here: "I will betroth you to myself with tenderness." Biblical commentaries are fond of using the Hebrew word, *hesed,* for faithfulness at this point. The basic meaning of the word is "bond," or "contract." If it is applied to human relationships, it takes on the meaning of loyalty. Hence, what is being said in this text, and indeed in the whole book of Hosea, is that God never ceases to be loyal to a people with whom He has pledged a contract.

No matter how faithless the people may be, no matter how often they may act like an adulteress, God remains loyal to His part of the covenant. And this is not just a passive loyalty, for He tries to woo them back to Him. He makes efforts to discover ways to win their hearts back to Himself.

It is true that God cannot bless His people, once they are faithless, but He always stands ready to grant His blessing, and He is anxious to grant it, once they are open to Him again. So if Hosea is to be remembered for anything, it should not be for just the story of his fickle wife, Gomer. Rather, it should be because he celebrates the *hesed,* the incredible loyalty of God to a solemn agreement He has made with man.

We may run after other gods and seek false prophets who satisfy our itching ears for new winds of doctrine. God, who has a patience befitting His wisdom, pursues a thousand ways to win us back. We can do no better than quote the final admonition of Hosea:

> "Whoever is wise, let him understand these things;
>   whoever is discerning, let him know them;
> for the ways of the Lord are right,
>   and the upright walk in them,
> but transgressors stumble in them" (Hosea 14:9).

The Coming of Jesus

Now that you have read about the patriarchs, kings, and prophets of Israel, I hope you have found in them the breath of God and a sense of His beauty and goodness. Rabbi Abraham Heschel once said, "I wait for the day when Christians will stop calling the Old Testament - old." Perhaps you now know what he means, because in so many ways it is as new as tommorrow's newspaper. Its message is as fresh as spring water and never fails to bring us near to God.

THE WORDS AND DEEDS OF JESUS

We turn now to the Holy Word as it appeared in messianic times. God comes near to us now in the remarkable person of Jesus Christ. We will take up the words and deeds of Jesus as they have come to us in the gospel. The reason for the special treatment of the birth and passion stories (*see* pages 181 and 188) is that the unique vision of the Gospel writers in these instances is so precious that I did not want to merge it with others. This would distract us from the directness of their message.

Again I have tried, wherever possible, to place for you a present day parallel to the event under consideration. No man's life has meant more to so many people in history than that of Jesus. Alone, among all those who ever lived, Jesus remains for all of us an incomparable person. Some have called Him ultimate man. In faith we name Him the Son of the living God. His story does not end with a death, but with a resurrection. Hence we who believe in Jesus do not simply look at Him as one who lived in the past, but as one who is spiritually present to us today.

BRINGING JESUS TO THE WORLD TODAY

To leave Jesus in a hall of fame is an infidelity to the meaning of the gospel. The story of Israel is sometimes called the Law or the *Torah*. Torah comes from a Hebrew root word that means "to help one to see." Hence Torah was meant to be the Law-light aiding us to see God. Jesus is the new torah, the new pillar of fire that lights the way to God in the New Time which He began at Jordan's bank.

Pierre Charles once wrote, "How can I see Jesus if I do not see Him in Christians?" Many felt that in the person of Pope John the world received a glimpse of Jesus. We can scarcely expect to make Jesus known to the world as Pope John did. But we can, each of us in his own small way, show that Jesus is truly present in the world today with all the power, hope, and love of His message.

The following presentation of the person of Jesus will, hopefully, be helpful in leading many of you who read it to doing just that, so that you become the Easter light to a world that too often prefers darkness. When that is true, then, indeed, the Good News has arrived.

SAINT MATTHEW'S STORY OF THE BIRTH OF JESUS
Jesus Is the Expected Messiah

Songs, lights, gift wrappings, smiles, ribbons, parties are part of the Christmas season in our culture. This is a season when the dream of Christian love becomes so real you can just about touch it. There is an ad that says, "A diamond is forever." The same is true of the meaning of Christmas. It introduces a spirit into our culture that, ultimately, will outlast the wars and human hate.

To discuss the meaning of Christmas we must turn to the record of the birth of Jesus. First we shall examine the account in Saint Matthew's Gospel, chapters 1 to 2, then the account in the Gospel of Saint Luke.

JESUS' FAMILY TREE

Matthew's account of Christ's birth is made up of six stories: the family tree (genealogy) of Jesus, Joseph's dilemma, the wise men, the flight into Egypt, the slaughter of the holy innocents, the joyous return.

The family tree of Jesus. The rootless man of today may not be turned on by family trees, so a look at the ancestors of Jesus can seem to be a tiresome reading assignment. Granted that few will find it exciting, let us still look at a few items of interest. There are three sets of fourteen names in the family tree. The name "David" was worth fourteen, that is, the letters for "David," in the Hebrews' number system, added up to fourteen. Possibly, one of the things Matthew wants us to understand is that Jesus is the new David. He wants to identify Jesus with the most loved public figure in Israel's memory. The family tree of Jesus is something like a cheerleading section shouting: "David! David! David!"

WHAT DOES THE FAMILY TREE SHOW US ABOUT CHRIST?

In addition, these three sets of fourteen names summarize the three main periods of Israel's history: the period of the patriarchs, the period of the kings, and the period after the exile. Jesus will give meaning to the patriarchal period as the new Moses, to the kingly time as one greater than David; to the period after the exile as the real Son of Man (see page 140). Lastly, the family tree shows that Jesus comes from a family of real people, and that He has a Jewish ancestry. The skeletons in the closet and the black sheep are there, including some of the least worthy kings of Judah. This is a case of history, "warts and all." And there is a sideline glance at Ruth, a Gentile girl among the Jewish women.

Joseph's dilemma. Joseph discovers that the girl he is about to marry is pregnant. Like any young husband, he is upset at this discovery. It takes a dream and a prophecy to calm him down. The angel of his dream assures Joseph that this is the work of the Spirit. The words of Isaiah confirm the dream, for Mary is the virgin who will conceive the Emmanuel-Child (Isaiah 7:14). This old prophecy had first been spoken to King Ahaz, who had been losing faith in God. He was assured of a son in whom God would dwell. The name "Emmanuel" means "God with us."

THE WISE MEN *visited the newborn Child and adored Him.
"Then, opening their treasures, they offered Him gifts of gold,
frankincense, and myrrh" (Matthew 2:11)*

THE STORY OF THE WISE MEN

The wise men. The story of the wise men has, out of devotion, been added to through the years. They are now pictured as being kings and, generally, numbered as three. The imagery of kings arises from a meditation on Psalm 72.

> "May the kings of Tarshish and the isles render
>   him tribute,
> may the kings of Sheba and Seba bring gifts!
> May all the kings fall down before him,
>   all nations serve him!"
>
> (Psalm 72:10–11).

The adoration of the wise men brings full meaning to the forecast that the nations would pay homage to the Messiah (*see* Isaiah 60:6). The wise men have come to be numbered as three because of the three gifts: gold, incense, and myrrh. The Fathers of the Church saw the gold as a sign of Christ's royalty, the incense as the mark of His divinity, and the myrrh as the indication of His passion and burial.

In this story, there is a star and a prophecy. The prophet Micah is recalled as the one who claimed the Messiah would be born in Bethlehem (*see* Micah 5:2). A mysterious star appears in the sky and, like a guiding angel, leads the wise men to the infant Jesus—the end of their quest.

The flight into Egypt. Matthew recounts Herod's threat to kill Jesus. Once again, a dream and a prophecy are the way of solution and survival. The angel warns Joseph in a dream, and the holy family goes into exile. Matthew sees in this God's way of giving fuller meaning to the old prophecy of Hosea: "Out of Egypt I called my son" (Hosea 11:1). The first son of God, Israel, had been called out of Egypt in the exodus (*see* page 59). Now, God's truest Son would do the same.

The slaughter of the holy innocents. The slaughter of some eighty babies in the vicinity of Bethlehem by a jealous king is one of the darker pages of history. Herod is so threatened by the thought of a rival king that he lashes out against the defenseless infants of a quiet town. There is no dream or angel, but there is a prophecy to accompany this story. "A voice was heard in Ramah, wailing and loud lamentation, Rachel weeping for her children; she refused to be consoled, because they were no more" (Matthew 2:18). Jewish history recalls Israel's national mourning, symbolized in the voice of Rachel, at the time of the great deportation of the Jews by the Assyrians, something similar to German Jews being loaded into boxcars by the Nazis and sent to the gas chambers at Treblinka. As Jeremiah put it, "Rachel is weeping for her children; she refuses to be comforted for her children, because they are not" (Jeremiah 31:15).

The joyous return. The death of the old tyrant Herod was a signal for the end of the holy family's exile. Again we have a dream and a prophecy. The angel of Joseph's dream announces the good news that they can go home, but that they should settle in Nazareth. A popular prophecy of the ancient times supports this move, the idea that the Messiah shall be called a Nazarene. There is no prophetic statement exactly like this. The birth story of Samson, in Judges 13:5, says that he is to be a Nazirite. But this does not refer to Nazareth. It is the title for men who followed a special type of spiritual discipline. It might be noted here that, in the early Church, the followers of Jesus were called Nazarenes in the Hebrew world. The Greek-Roman world called them Christians—the term that endured.

BIRTH OF JESUS LINKED TO TRADITIONAL JEWISH TEACHING

There are many details in Matthew's account that link Jesus to the person of Moses. The infant Moses survived when many innocent Hebrew children were drowned. Like Jesus, Moses went into exile at Midian. Moses led the son, Israel, out of Egypt. In this account, Herod is pictured as a new pharaoh. These links

MOSES *survived when many other innocent Hebrew children drowned—Jesus survived when Herod murdered the other innocent children. Many details in Matthew's account of Christ's birth link Jesus with the person of Moses*

with Moses, plus the prophecies and dream angels, are woven into a tight pattern so that the birth of Jesus is firmly linked to the traditional teaching of the Jews. It also shows Jesus as the one who brings final meaning to the Old Testament theology. Later on in Matthew, Jesus says He does not come to destroy the Torah, the law of the Old Testament, but to fulfill it.

To modern eyes, this may seem like a complicated code, too

troublesome to unravel. But to its first readers, this account was perfectly obvious. The story still tells us today that Jesus is our Lord and king. He survived violence, jealousy, and exile to bring us a vision and a hope of freedom.

SAINT LUKE'S STORY OF THE BIRTH OF CHRIST
A Report Gathered from Eyewitnesses

Reading Saint Luke's Christmas story, chapters 1 and 2, is like hearing the best-loved carols. It has the golden richness of an expensive Christmas card, the warmth of a Yule log, and the splendor of a midnight Mass. In all of biblical literature, Luke's Christmas story holds a unique place, both because of its poetic celebration of the birth of Jesus and its rich pattern of scriptural images.

THE INFLUENCE OF JEWISH THINKING AND MARY'S PRESENCE

To write his story, Luke consulted the traditional teachings of the apostolic community, most probably the testimony of the Virgin Mary. His research into the development of the apostolic preaching showed him that the original sermons clustered around the public life of Jesus. He detected the fourfold outline of: Jordan stories, Galilean ministry, journey to Jerusalem, and the death and resurrection of Jesus.

As Luke pored over the traditions, he noted that once the above outline was stabilized and accepted, the community began to gather data about the birth of Jesus. The elements of the birth story grew up in Judeo-Christian circles. The well-loved themes of the people of God, the temple, the cult and glory of Jerusalem, that appear in Luke's Gospel reflect a Jewish mentality, although Luke wrote in Greek.

An old tradition places Luke at Ephesus, where he would have had a chance to interview the Virgin Mary. Many have seen Luke's story as the poetic and exalted gospel which Mary, the virgin daughter of Zion, sang after she had contemplated this mystery in her heart over the years. She may have communicated this to Saint John, her guardian. Or she may have communicated it directly to Luke. At any rate, the story has the strong imprint of Jewish thinking together with the dominant presence of Mary. With this material, Luke presents us with his account of the origin of Jesus.

LUKE'S USE OF PARALLELS

One of the striking features of this narrative is Luke's use of numerous parallels. There are two annunciation scenes, one to Zechariah, the other to Mary. The birth story of John the Baptist is balanced by the birth story of Jesus. We have a visit of angels and then a visit of shepherds. Zechariah sings the *Benedictus* (Luke 1:68–79) to welcome his son John. Mary chants the beautiful *Magnificat* (Luke 1:46–55) to celebrate the approaching birth of Jesus. This use of parallels is a typical technique of Hebrew poetry. The Hebrew poets worked on this principle: never say anything once that you can say twice. A theme of growing anticipation moves through this parallel arrangement. The birth and manifestation of John the Baptist serves as a point of comparison and departure for the birth and manifestation of Jesus.

It may seem odd to us, but Luke was more impressed by the temple than the crib. It was not Christ's appearance in the stable

MARY *heard the angel say: "Behold, you will conceive in your womb and bear a son, and you shall call His name Jesus" (Luke 1:31)*

which caught Luke's imagination so much as His presentation in the temple. The first two chapters of Luke's Gospel are like a piece of music that gradually grows louder until it reaches its peak in Christ's being brought to the temple. "And when the time came for their purification according to the law of Moses, they brought him up to Jerusalem to present him to the Lord" (Luke 2:22).

STRIKING RESEMBLANCES BETWEEN DANIEL AND LUKE

On this point, Luke appears to be echoing the ninth and tenth chapters of the book of Daniel. There are striking resemblances between Daniel and Luke on this point. In chapter 9 of Daniel, the angel Gabriel appears to the prophet at the evening hour of sacrifice. Gabriel announces that seventy weeks of years will come before the dawn of the messianic era. The details of Gabriel's appearance to Daniel are very similar to the angel's visit to Zechariah. Both Daniel and Zechariah are filled with fear. Both are told to store in their hearts the information the angel gives them. There is even a similar loss of speech. "How can my lord's servant talk with my lord? For now no strength remains in me, and no breath is left in me" (Daniel 10:17).

Luke makes the seventy weeks of years from the book of Daniel into just plain seventy weeks. Between the angel's announcement to Zechariah that his wife, Elizabeth, will bear him a son and the angel's announcement to Mary that she will become the mother of Christ, six months of Elizabeth's pregnancy elapse. Then comes Mary's nine-month waiting period. And, from the birth of Jesus until His presentation in the temple, there is an interval of forty days. These three periods of time add up to 490 days. Using seven days in a week, this adds up to seventy weeks.

"Seventy weeks of years are decreed concerning your people and your holy city, to finish the transgression, to put an end to sin, and to atone for iniquity, to bring in everlasting righteousness, to seal both vision and prophet, and to anoint a most holy place" (Daniel 9:24). Luke says this is accomplished in seventy weeks, when Jesus comes to the temple, which is the most holy place.

HOPES OF THE PROPHETS REALIZED

Jesus comes to the temple to seal the hopes and visions of the prophets. The aged prophet, Simeon, comes forward and takes the holy child in his arms. With tears of joy, he proclaims that prophecy may now stop, since what was prophesied is now present. The old lady, Anna, comes to the temple and publicly expresses her thanks. Her thanks reflect the gratitude of the people of God, acknowledging that their waiting and hopes have not been in vain.

While the prophet Daniel supplies the overview for Luke's story, numerous other prophets offer themes which lend color and meaning to the Christmas story. Zephaniah paints the background canvas for the annunciation to Mary:

> "Sing aloud, O daughter of Zion;
>   shout, O Israel!
> Rejoice and exult with all your heart,
>   O daughter of Jerusalem!
> The Lord has taken away the judgments
>   against you . . .
> The King of Israel, the Lord, is in your
>   midst . . .
> On that day it shall be said to Jerusalem:
>   'Do not fear, O Zion. . . .' "
>
>   (Zephaniah 3:14–16).

The angels at Bethlehem sing of the glory. The word "glory" in Scripture is a way of speaking of the dynamic expression of God's presence and His radiant splendor (*see* page 143). It was this glory which overshadowed Mary and transformed her into an ark of the covenant.

MARY AND JOSEPH *arrive in Bethlehem. Mary may have personally told Luke the details of the story of Jesus' birth*

WHAT IS OUR CHALLENGE TODAY?

Luke uses the "echo technique" in telling the story of Jesus. By using carefully selected references to the Old Testament, Luke brilliantly shows that the birth of Jesus is the true fulfillment of the longings and hopes of Israel. He was faced with the problem of bringing home to the people of his time the real meaning of Jesus. This is a challenge that remains in our own time as well. It is not a job just for the theologians and preachers. It is the task of the whole Christian people. Such a work requires time and patience.

As Luke shows us, we must go beyond the crib to the temple. By all means, let us enjoy the wonder of a newborn baby, but we cannot be detained at the stable, no more than Jesus was. Jesus went on to the temple to anoint the holy place and seal the hopes of men. This, also, is our Christian task. We are to search into the riches of the mystery of religion to bring its promise of fulfillment to all those who wait and hope. On the holy night we hear the carol: "O come, all ye faithful!" We will join the liturgy of adoration, knowing that in the dawn we will bring this message of hope to our fellowmen.

A CALL FOR RENEWAL ON THE BANKS OF THE JORDAN

The Preaching of John the Baptist

Preparing for the Second Vatican Council, Pope John XXIII sent out his call from the banks of the Tiber summoning the Church to renew herself. Some years ago, a number of concerned national leaders stood before the Lincoln Memorial by the banks of the Potomac and called on the American people to change their hearts about civil rights for the Negro and other minority groups. And John the Baptist stood on Jordan's bank, shouting to Jerusalem and all Judea for a radical change of heart.

FOUR ELEMENTS IN THE JORDAN STORIES

There are four elements in the Jordan stories that need our attention here: (1) the Isaiah prophecy, chapters 40 to 66; (2) the judgment on the old Church; (3) the reply of the people; (4) the baptism of Jesus. Let's look at each of these.

The Isaiah prophecy. Today, when an American politician needs something to support his speeches, he turns to a familiar source – the Constitution. Just as a country's constitution is a favorite authority on political matters, so Isaiah was the favorite prophetic source for the Gospel writers. John the Baptist identified with the memory of Isaiah much the same as loyal Republicans today like to think of themselves as the party of Lincoln.

In the second half of the prophecy of Isaiah, chapters 40 to 66, the prophet consoled the Hebrew exiles in Babylon. Their seventy-year captivity was over and they would return to see the *glory* in the Holy Land. The joy of this historic return, however, would be but an image of the wonderful happiness that their descendants would know when the Savior would come to usher in the messianic age. Isaiah told of the herald of this good news – of the Messiah's coming – standing in the desert and calling for a preparation worthy of a king's arrival. In poetic language, the herald spoke of rolling away mountains and filling vast valleys to build a remarkable highway for the Lord.

GET READY FOR THE LORD

Now John the Baptist stands in the wilderness, which symbolizes the desert of the exodus and the Israelites' glorious victory over Egypt (*see* page 64). John becomes the herald of the good news and proclaims the arrival of the messianic age. Get ready for the Lord! The highway that must be built for the coming Lord is one of repentance. The hills of pride and the valleys of despair must be swept away so that we may be open to the Lord.

The Greek word for repentance is *metanoia.* Its basic meaning is "change." John's urgent call is not just for external penances, though these are not excluded, but for an interior change of the attitudes of the heart. John practices both. He lives on a diet that would put even a dieting girl to shame. Without embarrassment, he chooses the harsh wilderness. But for John, the external penances are a sign of the deep purification of his heart.

JESUS, *after His baptism by John in the Jordan, "saw the Spirit of God descending like a dove," and He heard a voice saying: "this is my beloved son, with whom I am well pleased"* (Matthew 3:16–17)

The judgment on the old Church. John's sermons were so rousing that he became the Billy Graham of his day. The poor and the proud came out in droves to hear him. John was in no mood for sweet talk and soft words. Far from praising his listeners' pious interest in sermons, he attacked their spiritual blindness.

"You brood of vipers! Who warned you to flee from the wrath to come? Bear fruits that befit repentance, and do not begin to say to yourselves, 'We have Abraham as our father'; for I tell you, God is able from these stones to raise up children to Abraham. Even now the axe is laid to the root of the trees" (Luke 3:7–9).

SHAKING UP THE COMFORTABLE

He accused them of turning the Church into a comfortable pew. Their religion had hardened into mere bones on which the Spirit did not breathe life and, like a dead old tree, it must be cut down. Indeed, the ax was already measuring the root. With such strong language, John attempted to shake them from their contentment with themselves.

The reply of the people. John burned a path into the hearts of his honest listeners. He led them to question the meaning of their lives. On all sides, the cry arose: "What shall we do?" John aroused a sense of justice in the people. He bade the wealthy give food and clothing to the poor. He urged tax agents to renounce all crooked practices. He urged soldiers to refrain from armed robbery, and to learn how to be content with their army pay (*see* Luke 3:10–14). John pleaded for a moral change like that preached by the great prophets. This change of heart and behavior is the best preparation for the arrival of the Lord.

CREATION STORY AND ISAIAH'S SERVANT SONGS RECALLED

The baptism of Jesus. The fourth element of the Jordan story is the appearance of the Lord Himself. As the humble servant of

JOHN THE BAPTIST, *announcing the coming of the Lord, preached the need for repentance: the people must undergo a change of heart*

the Father, Jesus comes to the Jordan to be anointed Messiah. The baptismal scene combines both the creation story of Genesis, chapter 1 (*see* page 15), and the teaching of the servant songs of Isaiah (especially chapter 42:1–4) (*see* page 140).

The creation story is recalled in the story of Jesus' baptism by the image of the dove and the river. In Genesis, creation is brought out of the dark watery chaos by the power of the Spirit (breath) of God (*see* page 16). This Spirit hovers over the chaos like a dove. The Jordan is now the chaos and, above it, is the Spirit of God confirming Jesus as the minister of the new creation. The new age is now to begin.

This scene also recalls the first of the servant songs of Isaiah. "Behold my servant, whom I uphold, ["This is my beloved Son . . ."] my chosen, in whom my soul delights; [". . . with whom I am well pleased."] I have put my Spirit upon him, [the Spirit appears above Jesus in the form of a dove] he will bring forth justice [a description of Jesus' messianic role] to the nations." Compare Isaiah 42:1 and Matthew 3:16–17. They show the remarkable parallel between the servant song and the baptism of Jesus.

JESUS BRINGS FULL MEANING TO JOHN'S TEACHING

At the Jordan, Jesus brings full meaning to the teaching of John. Jesus makes the dreams of the poor and humble come true. He establishes forever a vision that rescues the hopeless from despair. The best news of all is not just that He is dedicated to working for justice for all, but that He will make men just. Through His passion and resurrection, Jesus will enable men to be released from the heavy burden of guilt and sin that causes them so much anxiety. The saving work of Jesus will give men a sense of being just. This is not a self-righteous justice, born of false piety, but a humble and honest justice proceeding from God Himself.

The season of Advent celebrates the Jordan baptism. All Christians again go down to Jordan to hear the plea for change, the reminder that the ax is laid to the root. In their hearts, the old questions about the meaning of their lives and about justice arise once more. And there is Jesus' blessed promise that we need weep no more.

JESUS IS A REAL MAN
Christ's Humanity

It is an interesting feature of our times that we must make sure our heroes are really *men*. Robert Bolt named Sir Thomas More, "A Man For All Seasons." Dale Wasserman called the idealistic knight, Don Quixote, "The Man of La Mancha." We can grant their godlike qualities more easily if we can be assured they were *men*. Ted Williams is enrolled in baseball's Hall of Fame, but his fans do not forget his blazing *human* skills in the game.

The same is true of Jesus. No Gospel is stronger in celebrating the lofty divinity of Jesus than Saint John's. Yet it is equally insistent that He was a real *man*. Saint John's first chapter gives us a series of five testimonies about Jesus which underline His human qualities. These five testimonies are given by: John the Baptist, Andrew, Philip, Nathanael, and Christ Himself.

JESUS IS THE SUFFERING SERVANT

We hear first from the trumpetlike voice of the prophet, John the Baptist. He drew the attention of his congregation to Jesus and declared: "Behold, the Lamb of God." The Aramaic word John used here was *talya,* a word that means both lamb and servant. When the audience seated along Jordan's bank heard this expression, they remembered the Old Testament poetry about the suffering servant of Yahweh (*see* page 140).

These poems in the book of Isaiah speak of a mysterious man who will come one day to bring justice to all nations. He will be called, simply, the "servant." However, his work will summon him to suffer for the sins of men. He will be led like a lamb to the slaughter. Through this purifying suffering, men will be redeemed.

Hence, John presents Jesus as the servant-lamb who has come to be the man for others and who is dedicated, even to death, for the cause of man's salvation. The Church today is striving to come nearer to this ideal. You hear more often now about the "servant Church." Like Jesus, the Church works to establish justice on the earth. And like Jesus, it is pledged to insure that justice.

JESUS IS THE MESSIAH

The second testimony comes from Andrew, the brother of Simon Peter. Andrew had stood on the Jordan's bank with the crowd that heard John the Baptist call Jesus "the Lamb of God." He found himself compelled to find out more about this man. Together with a friend, he approached Jesus and asked to stay with Him for awhile. "They stayed with Him that day, for it was about the tenth hour" (John 1:39). Andrew was so impressed that he rushed back to his brother Simon Peter and said, "We have found the Messiah" (John 1:41).

Andrew called Jesus the Messiah because he sensed in this man a religious teaching that really saves. He had listened to many men speak, and in his heart quietly asked, "Do you have a message that can really save me? Can you speak to my loneliness? Are you a teacher who knows how to bring meaning to my life? Can you really tell me who I am?" In Jesus he found that the answer was a resounding yes!

The Church today struggles anew to continue this messianic promise of Jesus. The world questions the Church as Andrew questioned Jesus. And in word and sacrament, the Church works to bring men a religion that really saves them.

TRUE MEANING OF RELIGIOUS STUDY

We hear the third testimony from Philip who came from Bethsaida. He told his friend Nathanael: "We have found him of whom Moses in the law and also the prophets wrote, Jesus of Nazareth, the son of Joseph" (John 1:45). The word "law" here refers to the Torah, that is, the first five books of the Bible. Two of the main sources of theology for an Israelite were the Torah and the prophets.

Philip spoke here as a student. He had studied his theology well and had lived by it with honesty. His studies, together with his deep faith, had given him an understanding of the work of God in the world. He was familiar with the mighty deeds of the God of the exodus and the dreams of the prophets. This was why his encounter with Jesus was such an experience, for this man bore in His person a mighty breakthrough of the power of God and the vision of which all the prophets had spoken.

Because of this, Philip is a patron of the student of religion. He is a reminder that religious studies are avenues to meeting the Lord Jesus. They are not meant to be a detached, academic work, but an opening to love and service in the name of Jesus.

SON OF GOD AND KING OF ISRAEL

Our fourth testimony is delivered by Nathanael. He is best known for saying, "Can anything good come out of Nazareth?" Jesus said that Nathanael was a man in whom there was no guile. In other words Nathanael was an "innocent abroad," an honest man who felt no need to resort to tricks in his human relations. When he was brought to meet Jesus, he announced: "Rabbi, you are the Son of God! You are the King of Israel!" (John 1:49).

JESUS *is a real man who brings meaning to the lives of all men*

These two statements are Old Testament religious declarations. The expression "Son of God" was not a reference to personal divinity, but a way of saying how close this person was to God. Of course, eventually Nathanael would come to know the deeper truth of this statement when applied to Jesus. "King of Israel" was a technical expression meaning the messianic spiritual leader of the people of God.

Because Nathanael was an open man, the impact of Jesus was so great that Nathanael clearly saw the role of Christ. Really knowing Christ requires this directness which is the mark of a genuine person. It helps to be "without guile."

CHRIST'S OWN TESTIMONY: HE IS THE COVENANT MAN

The final testimony comes from the lips of Jesus Himself. He addressed it to Nathanael: "Truly, truly, I say to you, you will see heaven opened, and the angels of God ascending and descending upon the Son of man" (John 1:51). Note two elements in Jesus' testimony: activity of the angels and "Son of man." They refer to two Old Testament dreams. Chapter 28 of Genesis tells the story of Jacob's dream at Bethel. There, a ladder appeared on his chest and angels climbed up and down on it between God and Jacob. God renewed His covenant with the patriarch (*see* page 45). Here, Jesus is saying that the angels ascend and descend upon Him. He is now the real covenant man.

In chapter 7 of Daniel, we are told of a dream Daniel had in which a black lake appears over which blow four winds. Four unspeakable monsters emerge from the lake. This is an image of the first creation from which came the monstrous old Adam who tyrannized the earth. God condemns this old mankind and looks for another. Across the skies in the clouds of heaven, comes a son of man who looks into the face of God. To him is given the new creation, because he is a genuine man whose promise to be the image of God will really happen (*see* page 166).

JESUS THE MESSIAH *called James and John to His service and told them He would make them "fishers of men"*

Jesus declares that He is this man spoken of in Daniel's dream. He has come to found a new mankind. He is a new Adam who will not tyrannize the earth, but work it for the sake of human concern. Jesus says of Himself, therefore, that He is the covenant man. His purpose and the will of God will merge so that the divine promise for the earth will be fulfilled.

Hence, the testimonies that bear witness to Jesus and His meaning for us are: servant-lamb, Messiah, true meaning of religious study, Son of God and King of Israel, covenant man. An understanding of these testimonies sets the stage for an understanding of Jesus as a real man. It will also open us to see His glory, for in Him, as in no other man, God broke through for all men to see.

THE WEDDING FEAST AT CANA AND THE CLEANSING OF THE TEMPLE

Signs of God's Presence Among Men

A great man evokes the uncanny feeling that he shows something beyond himself. Indeed when we read the lives of the great men and women of history who dedicated themselves to the betterment of their fellowmen, we see that all of them, in one way or another, went "beyond themselves." Jesus was a real man, the greatest man in history, and the "beyond" broke through Him in an incomparable way. Saint John says that in Jesus he saw the "glory."

"THE GLORY"

In the Old Testament the word "glory" was associated with images of the pillar of fire, the radiant cloud, the roaring wind at Sinai, the gentle whisper at Carmel, the burning bush at Horeb, and the breath of God that fluttered like a dove over the waters of chaos in Genesis. In other words, *glory* summed up the variety of Old Testament religious experiences of the living God among the children of men.

To speak of the glory breaking through the person of Jesus is a way of saying that the divine presence was profoundly experienced by those who knew and loved Jesus. Chapters 2-4 of John's Gospel present an image of Jesus performing signs of the divine breakthrough. John records two events, the miracle of the wine at Cana and the cleansing of the temple, and follows these with two conversations that illuminate the meaning of the events. We shall discuss the events of Cana and the temple.

THE WEDDING FEAST AT CANA: ITS MEANING

"On the third day there was a marriage at Cana in Galilee, and the mother of Jesus was there" (John 2:1). This tightly packed sentence has three major ideas that give us a clue to the meaning of the Cana story. First, the expression "third day" is a biblical way of speaking of a radically new experience. It has an Easter quality about it. Something entirely new was about to happen.

Second, the portrait of a wedding feast is the Bible's way of talking about the age of glorious happiness. In our terms, it is a way of speaking about heaven. A banquet was one of the most joyful things the biblical writers knew. Adding a wedding made it the summit of happiness imagery. These people had been taught that when the Messiah came to usher in the new age, it would be like an everlasting wedding dinner.

The third detail is the presence of Mary. She arrives as the woman who has summed up in herself the faith of Israel by uttering the great *Amen* to God. Jesus, as the new Adam, comes with Mary, the new Eve, to Cana, that there, as Man and Woman, they may announce the new age in the atmosphere of a messianic banquet.

JESUS, *at the wedding feast, changed the water into wine.*
"This, the first of His signs, Jesus did at Cana in Galilee, and
manifested His glory; and His disciples believed in Him"
(John 2:11)

The giant water jars represent the purification rituals of the Old Testament. They symbolize the supremacy of the law in the Old Testament search for salvation. Jesus replaces this water with wine. The river of wine is a sign of the new blessings of salvation brought by Christ, namely through the power of the Spirit. The law washed only the outside of a man, as water removed the dust from his feet. The Spirit expands the heart of man with love and freedom as wine loosens and rejoices the inner man.

The prophet Amos hinted at this when he said: "Behold, the days are coming . . . when the plowman shall overtake the reaper and the treader of grapes him who sows the seed; *the mountains shall drip sweet wine,* and all the hills shall flow with it" (Amos 9:13). John's comment about Cana is brief: "This, the first of his signs, Jesus did at Cana in Galilee, and manifested his glory; and his disciples believed in him" (John 2:11).

THE CLEANSING OF THE TEMPLE

Right on the heels of the Cana story comes the narrative about the cleansing of the temple. Jesus appears as an angry, menacing prophet bent on purifying the Church. The story makes more sense when seen against the background of five Old Testament pictures.

First: Isaiah 1:10–18 — The prophet Isaiah delivers a sermon in the temple area to a well-fed and hypocritical audience. He tells them that God hates their liturgy, no matter how well done, because they are a selfish, unjust, and unconcerned people. God is only pleased with worship by people who seek justice and live honestly in their daily lives.

Second: Jeremiah 7:11 — The prophet Jeremiah stands at the doorway of the temple scolding the people for mere externalism in their worship, and for turning the holy place into a *den of robbers.* Like Adam, who stole the forbidden fruit, they rob the temple of the real meaning of worship.

Third: Zechariah 14:21 — Commenting on the messianic age,

the prophet Zechariah foresees that the gross materialism of worship will be purged away. "And there shall no longer be *a trader* in the house of the Lord of hosts on that day."

Fourth: Psalm 69 — Here is a liturgical song about a just man who dedicated himself to the purification of the Church. He has already experienced the suffering which such work has brought upon him. "For zeal for thy house has consumed me." It is a task that leads to suffering and even to death.

Fifth: Malachi 3:1–5 — "The Lord whom you seek will suddenly come to his temple . . . he will purify the sons of Levi [the clergy] and refine them like gold and silver, till they present right offerings to the Lord."

These five passages form the spirit and content of the meaning of the temple cleansing. Jesus rails against the liturgy of the apparently just, accuses them of making the temple a den of thieves, drives out the traders, and opens Himself to the threat of death. He destroys the temple, that is, the old way of worship, and replaces it with Himself as both lamb and priest to offer a new and acceptable worship to the Father.

TWO EVENTS WITH AN IMPORTANT MESSAGE

The wedding feast at Cana and the cleansing of the temple are, then, two events with an important message for us. Jesus brings a new law and a new liturgy. Instead of legalism, He presents us with the freedom of the Spirit. Instead of a building full of selfish and hypocritical people, He offers us a worship that should grow out of a community blessed by the Spirit and filled with a record of works of love and concern.

These are signs of the glory, of the breakthrough of the divine, in the person of Jesus. These signs are works of terrifying majesty. They are public events that onlookers cannot avoid. The river of wine is a challenge to salvation by mere external performance of the law. The temple cleansing is a deliberate threat to all efforts

JESUS CLEANSING THE TEMPLE *teaches us that God is only pleased with worship by people who seek justice and live honestly in their daily lives*

to reduce worship to mere ritual performed by a self-righteous congregation.

The consecration of the wine at Mass recalls for us the marvel of Cana. The appearance of the new wine on the table of the Lord is our blessed assurance that Jesus lives on to give us freedom to develop as real persons, and to help others to sense this gift. Liturgical and social reform together with prophetic sermons are modern forms of the temple cleansing, reminding us to be truly just, not merely to give the appearance of being just.

In these ways Christ, who lives on in His Church, continues to teach today the message He taught at the wedding feast in Cana and at the cleansing of the temple.

FOLLOWING CHRIST MEANS PUTTING YOUR LIFE ON THE LINE
The Challenge of the Truly Christian Life

"Show me your friends and I'll tell you the kind of man you are." This old saying has taken on the modern twist of "guilt by association." Ever since the McCarthy hearings of the 1950's, which dealt with communist infiltration in high government places, the popular notion of someone being a security risk has developed. We not only avoid a man because we disagree with him, but also to escape being identified with his cause, be it communism or pacifism or neo-Nazism.

JESUS WAS A SECURITY RISK

The only thing new about this idea is the phrasing. Jesus was a security risk to the people of His time. He presented a special problem to the theologians who were the defenders of the established religion and the custodians of its truth and practices. Jesus became a threat to them because His teachings were radically different and often opposed to theirs.

Because they were so deeply threatened by what He had to say, the religious leaders found themselves unable to listen to Him without prejudice. To them, He was simply a heretic. They judged Him to be unworthy of serious discussion. They saw Him as so far out that the best they could say of Him was that He was a religious crank; and the worst, that He was a blasphemer. His message was a disturbance to the simple faith of the people and a danger to their cautious relations with the Roman embassy at the Fortress Antonia. To be seen with Him publicly would be a security risk.

One of these men, however, was honest enough to recognize real worth in the teachings of Jesus. His name was Nicodemus. He was a timid man, afraid to risk his reputation by being seen with Jesus in public. So, he arranged a meeting with Jesus in the middle of the night. The story is told in the third chapter of Saint John's Gospel.

DOES NICODEMUS TRULY UNDERSTAND?

Nicodemus began the discussion by declaring that he thinks Jesus is a true prophet of the living God. "Rabbi, we know that you are a teacher come from God; for no one can do these signs that you do, unless God is with him" (John 3:2). Nicodemus has read correctly the signs of the glory which shone through Jesus at the Cana miracle and the cleansing of the temple (*see* page 208).

Jesus replied that Nicodemus must undergo a profound change if he is to truly grasp the meaning of His work. This, so far, Nicodemus does not fully understand. Nicodemus must, first, be seized by the Spirit of God, that he may begin to understand and enter into a new way of life.

Such is the meaning of Christ's words: "Truly, truly, I say to you, unless one is born anew, he cannot see the kingdom of God . . . unless one is born of water and the Spirit, he cannot enter the kingdom of God" (John 3:3, 5). In other words: unless you are made to understand by the powerful breath which is the Spirit of God, you will not change and, therefore, cannot enter the new way of life.

HOW MAY WE HAVE ETERNAL LIFE?

This language is in keeping with the creation theme of the early chapters of John. The creation stories of the Old Testament are dominated by the two images of the dark lake and the breath-Spirit of God. Nicodemus has to be brought out of the dark lake of chaos and misunderstanding and led by the powerful breath of the Holy Spirit to an understanding of the meaning of Christ (*see* page 16). The words Jesus addressed to Nicodemus also refer to the sacrament of baptism which is the public sign and consecration of that interior conversion of which Jesus speaks.

Nicodemus asked how this can come about. Jesus is not above a

NICODEMUS *was a timid man, and did not want to risk his reputation by being seen with Jesus in public*

little humor at this point. He teased Nicodemus about being a teacher of religion who should know better. "Are you a teacher of Israel and yet do not understand this?" (John 3:10). Jesus then reminded Nicodemus of the old story of Moses and the bronze serpent, the tale of the griping Israelites forever complaining about the water shortage and the poor diet. The Lord punished the people by sending fiery serpents among them. They bit the people and many died.

The people repented and prayed for mercy. God instructed Moses to make a bronze serpent and put it on a pole. The pole symbolized majesty and God's power over the serpent, which was itself a symbol of sinful religious practices. All who looked upon the up-raised figure were healed (*see* Numbers 21:4–9). Jesus then made the application of the story: "So must the Son of Man be lifted up, that whoever believes in him may have eternal life" (John 3:14). Jesus, as the new mankind, the Son of Man, must be raised up to the cross and to glory so that the reality Nicodemus searches for may come to pass.

THE WORK OF THE TRINITY

Jesus then went on to speak to Nicodemus about His Father. The Father has given the world His Son that it might discover the way to true manhood. The Father presents His Son to the world as a sign of judgment: "He who believes in him is not condemned" (John 3:18). Further, the Father commands that the followers of Jesus must do their deeds in the light. This means that the Christian must always be open and honest. "But he who does what is true comes to the light, that it may be clearly seen that his deeds have been wrought in God" (John 3:21).

In effect, Jesus is telling Nicodemus that the work of the new creation is wrought by the Holy Trinity. The Spirit works mightily to draw men out of the chaos (*see* John 3:1–8). This is made possible through the death and resurrection of the Son (*see* John 3:9–15). And all this is set in motion by the immense love of the heavenly Father (*see* John 3:16–21).

BAPTISM IS A SIGN OF A CHANGE OF HEART

The majority of Bible commentators stress the reference to baptism in this story: "unless one is born of water and the Spirit. . . ." But in their eagerness to support the sacrament of baptism as necessary for salvation, they bypass the richer meaning of these texts, especially Christ's call for a radical change of life as necessary for baptism. For Christ, the event of baptism is the sign of an interior commitment.

Hence, the primary emphasis is on the *change of heart*. The liturgical ceremony of baptism is a celebration and public announcement of this basic change. It is a proclamation that the candidate is ready to follow Jesus through the cross to glory. It is his public commitment to be a man.

The real risk in associating with Jesus is this: what He promises can happen. He asks us to put our life on the line in order to find meaning and happiness. Do we want to do it?

THE SAMARITAN WOMAN

Jesus Gives Meaning to her Life

Nobody likes a phony. Unmasking the hypocrite gives us great satisfaction. To a certain extent, everyone has a cover story that eventually should be stripped away so that the true person may emerge. John the Evangelist, in the fourth chapter of his Gospel, tells the story of how Jesus helped the Samaritan woman remove her mask and achieve the honesty that brought her salvation.

THE ANCIENT HOSTILITY BETWEEN JEW AND SAMARITAN

This story must be read against the background of an ancient hostility between the Jews and the Samaritans. After the death of King Solomon there was a civil war in Israel. The northern tribes broke away from the south and formed a separate kingdom. The capital of this new nation was Samaria. Consequently, the inhabitants of this northern nation gradually became known as Samaritans (*see* page 114).

The war also produced a religious division. The kings of the north forbade their subjects to worship at the temple in Jerusalem. Instead they provided a shrine for their people at the summit of Mount Gerizim. The passing years deepened the political and religious differences between the Jews and the Samaritans to the point where open hatred was commonplace.

JESUS MEETS THE SAMARITAN WOMAN

As this story opens, Jesus and His apostles are making a trip to Galilee. A quick way to get there was through Samaria. They paused by the well of Jacob. The well was situated between the holy mountain, Gerizim, and the mountain of the curse, named Ebal. The village of Sychar was just up the road. It was noontime, and Jesus was tired and hungry. He remained at the well to rest while His apostles went into the village to get some food.

Then "there came a woman of Samaria to draw water. Jesus said to her, 'Give me a drink' " (John 4:7). This is the theme of the "cup of water." To give a cup of water to even the least of one of our brothers is to give it to Jesus and to find ourselves on the road to salvation (Matthew 10:42). We also have here a case of Jesus not being recognized, for the woman has no idea of who He is, other than the fact that He is a Jew.

The Samaritan woman expressed her surprise that a male Jew would dare to ask a favor of her. He told her that He would give her *living* water. Compare this expression with the *living* bread Jesus would speak of in the sixth chapter of John (*see* page 232). Living water is *running* water, in contrast to a still, stagnant pool. In a desert land like Palestine, running water was a valued commodity and a symbol of life. In a sense, the woman is the parched earth, and Jesus has come to bring the refreshing waters of salvation to her arid spirit.

The woman remarked that it would hardly be possible for Jesus to give her water because He had no rope or bucket, and she asked Him if He thought He was greater than Jacob, who gave this well to the people. Jesus overlooked her sarcasm and assured her that the water He would give her would be such that she would never thirst again.

JESUS PROBES FOR THE TRUTH

To a certain extent, this appealed to her selfish nature. She would no longer need to haul water if what He said were true. "Go, call your husband," Jesus told her (John 4:16). With this command, Jesus struck at her cover story. He confronted her with her behavior. She insisted that she had no husband. But Jesus pursued the point, declaring that she had had five husbands, and so the man she now lived with was not her husband.

Never in her life had she felt so embarrassed. The truth that Jesus confronted her with was so painful that she quickly searched for a way of changing the subject. Rather than discuss her personal life, she switched the trend of conversation to a discussion of religion.

She told Jesus that she could see He was a prophet, and she asked Him which was the best place to worship. Was real religion to be found at the temple on Mount Zion in Jerusalem, or at the Samaritan shrine on Mount Gerizim? Jesus patiently took up her question and discussed it.

"Woman, believe me, the hour is coming when neither on this mountain nor in Jerusalem will you worship the Father. . . . But the hour is coming, and now is, when the true worshipers will worship the Father in spirit and truth" (John 4:21, 23). In other words, *today* you can worship as one born new by the Spirit. Today you can worship in truth, that is, with an openness and honesty never known before. Worship is not so much a matter of holy spaces or buildings as it is a matter of the honesty of the heart.

He had finally reached her. She frankly admitted that she was in need of help. Wistfully, she talked of the contemporary hope for a savior who would bring meaning and hope to women such

THE SAMARITAN WOMAN *said to Jesus: "How is it that you, a Jew, ask a drink of me, a woman of Samaria?" (John 4:9)*

as she. With that, Jesus revealed His identity and said, "I who speak to you am he" (John 4:26).

THE WOMAN RECEIVES CHRIST'S MESSAGE WITH JOY

Alleluia! Great excitement took hold of the woman. Without another word she rose and ran into the town to tell everyone that she had met a man who had given meaning to her life and who had filled her with hope. She ran to spread the gospel of peace and she became the first evangelist to the Samaritans.

The apostles returned just at the moment that the woman, with burning eyes, rushed past them. They wondered what had happened between her and Jesus. Jesus now seemed so absorbed that their presence was an intrusion. Bashfully they offered Him food. He looked at them and asked them how they could talk of food when He had just saved a woman. How could they think of lunch when He had just brought spiritual renewal to a woman whose life had been meaningless? He drew their attention to the grain fields. The tips of the wheat were white gold and ready for the harvest. He showed them that this is the symbol of the fullness of time when the whole world is ripe for His saving words and deeds. There no longer had to be a sense of being lost, for the inrush of His power had begun the saving task.

The scene closed with the arrival of the villagers of Sychar who came to hear the good news from the lips of Jesus Himself. Their testimony was a confession of faith: "We have heard for ourselves, and we know that this is indeed the savior of the world" (John 4:42).

Centuries before, there was an intimation of what would happen at the well of Jacob in a hymn composed by the prophet Isaiah:

"With joy you will draw water from the wells of
salvation. And you will say in that day:

Give thanks to the Lord,
        call upon his name;
make known his deeds among the nations,
        proclaim that his name is exalted. . . .
Shout and sing for joy, O inhabitant of Zion,
        for great in your midst is the
        Holy One of Israel" (Isaiah 12:3–4, 6).

THE COMFORTING WORD

Christ's Love and Concern for Mankind

Public words these days are not always comforting. Men in high places talk more openly about the third world war. University campuses are filled with strife and sharp debate. Civil-rights people complain that the legislation in their favor is poorly applied and carelessly executed. The old Church complains about the new Church. Teenagers are under fire for their fads, clothes, dances, and songs. It's a grim picture if we pay attention only to the loudest voices.

MIRACLES SHOW GOD'S LOVE

Where can we find the comforting word? Who speaks with hope and not just with discord, tension, conflict, and hate? The Bible remarks: How beautiful are the feet of those who bring the gospel of peace (*see* Romans 10:15).

Jesus brings the comforting word. It is He who brought history the gospel of peace. Take the story of the cure of the nobleman's son in the fourth chapter of Saint John's Gospel. A prominent nobleman asks Jesus to come and cure his son who is at the point of death. At first Jesus delays, discussing the people's desire to have signs and wonders in order to believe.

In other words, the people are looking for miracles so that they might believe. But Jesus wants them to see the miracles as a breakthrough of God's love, a demonstration of divine concern. Miracles are not to be a proof of faith, but a call to faith. It is not a matter of having miracles to support faith. Rather, God makes Himself personally present in the mighty deed. Faith here is the decision to believe that it is really He, and to say "amen" to His awesome presence.

In John's Gospel, the miracles are usually called signs. They are manifestations of the glory (*see* page 272). They are a summons to faith, not a proof of it. They are invitations to commitment, not arguments to defend God.

But note that the nobleman is too upset to argue the theology of miracles. That is for the scholar. His son is dying. He awaits the comforting word. "Sir, come down before my child dies" (John 4:49).

JESUS GIVES THE COMFORTING WORD

Jesus delays no longer. He ends the discussion of the meaning of miracles. He is caught up in the personal problem of an anguished father. He pronounces the life-giving word: ". . . 'Go; your son will live.' The man believed the word that Jesus spoke to him and went his way. And as he was going down, his servants met him and told him that his son was living" (John 4:50–51).

Take a similar story in Matthew 15:21–28. Jesus and the apostles are on their way through the district of Tyre and Sidon. This is pagan land. A Gentile woman approaches the group and asks help for her daughter who is plagued by a demon. The apostles form around Jesus to keep the woman from bothering Him. It's much the same as a secretary who protects the boss from troublesome clients.

The woman pushes her way past them and kneels at the feet

JESUS *said to Jairus' daughter: "Little girl, I say to you, arise. And immediately the girl got up and walked" (Mark 5:41–42). Jesus used miracles to show us God's concern for mankind.*

JESUS *wanted us to see His miraculous healing of the sick as a breakthrough of God's love, a demonstration of divine concern*

of Jesus. She repeats her plea in the cry that characterizes all the suffering people of this world: "Lord, help me" (Matthew 15:25). Jesus tells her that it is not right to take the bread of the children and give it to dogs.

What Jesus means by this remark is that His mission is to work among the Jews, not the pagans. But the woman probes deeper than the strict law or logic. "Yes, Lord, yet even the dogs eat the crumbs that fall from their master's table" (Matthew 15:27). She challenges Jesus to go beyond the strict demands of the law and let the beauty of His love and mercy shine forth.

Jesus had said that the poor are to be blessed because they are now to inherit the kingdom of God. The woman's heartfelt plea to Him is a call to let this kingdom overflow into the shattered life of her sick daughter. And she hears the comforting word: "O woman, great is your faith! Be it done for you as you desire" (Matthew 15:28). And her daughter is healed instantly.

WHERE DO WE FIND THE COMFORTING WORD TODAY?

The special place of the comforting word today is the sacrament of penance. It is the focus of gentleness in the Church. This can be seen in the great text on forgiveness of sins in John's Gospel, chapter 20. Here, the Easter Lord comes through the door of the upper room and greets His followers with the word "shalom." This is a Hebrew word that means peace and blessing. Jesus goes on to tell the disciples that they now have the power to forgive sins. He illustrates for them the attitude they should have in the sacrament of penance. They are to be judges, not sitting above the penitent, but gently making place for the shalom-love and mercy of Christ. Jesus shows them His wounds, thus affirming that He shared the burden of sin on the cross.

He reminds them that they are not to control the penitent, but to present the reality of Christ and His grace. They are not to do anything "dis-graceful." Hence, confession will be a sacrament announcing to the Church that the warm peace of Christ has taken hold of the penitent.

THE LIVING BREAD
The Meaning of the Eucharist

Perhaps no one can be hungrier than a teenager. Teenagers love to eat, not just for survival or to go on living, but also for pleasure and growth. It sometimes takes a miracle of bread to satisfy them, but there is no question of their hunger.

Jesus performed a miracle of bread, not only to still the pangs of physical hunger in the crowd of five thousand, but also to meet their spiritual hunger (John 6:1–15). Spiritual hunger can mean many things. The man who is starved for beauty knows such hunger. The girl who craves love understands spiritual hunger. The boy who yearns for justice and recognition has a clue to this hunger. The scholar who searches for meaning has a spiritual hunger.

JESUS BRINGS US HOPE

Jesus thought of this hunger when He multiplied the loaves. In this miracle, He began His work to satisfy the spiritual hunger of men and brought it to full realization in the Eucharist. At the Mass, beauty, love, recognition, and meaning all have their place. The early Church loved to call the Mass the "breaking of the bread." At this holy meal, Jesus celebrates with His friends their various searches, whether these be for dignity in place of squalor in the slums, or for a real friend in a lonely world.

Jesus blesses this search. Through communion with Him, our striving takes on more meaning. We are assured that our quest is not a waste of time. His presence to us is an invitation to move ahead. He tells us to have hope in action.

THE EUCHARIST: A SIGN OF COMMUNITY

One of the spiritual hungers most often spoken of today is the yearning for community. Artists picture us as huddled together on a dust heap like ants on a mound. They say we are a group but we do not communicate with one another. There is no real communion. Guidance counselors often hear teenagers complain they can't communicate with their parents. Even in so intimate a group as the family, communication often breaks down.

Jesus intended the Eucharist to be a sign of community. "Holy Communion" is not just the union of Jesus and the individual, but also the union we have with one another. Ideally, it is not a meal of strangers, but of friends. If this is so, then the Eucharistic event should have community-forming details about it.

We can find hints of this in the miracle of the loaves and fish, recorded in John, chapter 6. After telling of the miracle, John recalls for us the "Bread of life sermon." First, Jesus has a conversation with the people. They ask Him questions about His origins. They want to know what kind of works they should do in order to satisfy their hopes.

Conversation is the simplest and most human way of beginning to form a community. After all, a community is a group of friends. And one of the ways that people become friends is to tell each other about themselves and to exchange ideas. So Jesus employs this basic approach to form these strangers into friends – to make them into a community.

FORMING A COMMUNITY AT MASS

Where circumstances permit, this can sometimes be done at our Mass today by what is called the dialogue homily. This is a sermon in which the preacher invites the people to express themselves about the faith. He encourages them to make applications of faith to daily life. He supports their efforts to communicate their deep feelings to the others so that a human community will be formed.

After the conversation, Jesus talks about the manna the Israelites ate during the exodus (*see* page 68). Since there is no more manna from the desert days, He must be talking about a

JESUS *instituted the Eucharist as a sacrament through which we are not only united to Him but also to one another*

new kind of manna. By manna Jesus now means wisdom. He claims to be the living manna, or what we would say, living wisdom. How does this help to form community?

Wisdom can be an "out" word to some people. Perhaps a better word is "meaning." You cannot have community if there is no reason to be together. A community is pointless if there is no meaning to bind the members together. When Jesus speaks of Himself as the living wisdom, He is saying that He is the source of meaning for the group. He gives them a teaching that will bring them true hope and happiness. His person is a rallying point for unity.

FORMING A COMMUNITY BY THE
SACRAMENT OF THE EUCHARIST

Jesus is no puzzle to His listeners once they decide that it is all right to trust Him. It is a decision that includes a risk. They will only know His true meaning after they have committed themselves to Him. Jesus promises them that He will make them really live in the present time, and that this life will continue in the world to come. "Every one who sees the Son and believes in him should have eternal life; and I will raise him up at the last day" (John 6:40).

Now we see that Jesus forms the people into a community by inviting them into a deep conversation and by giving meaning to the group. He continues this work of forming community by introducing the sacrament. To reach community at its most basic level they must eat the bread and drink the cup. They are to eat His body and drink His blood. This union will mean that they have met their Lord in a profound, personal, and living way.

When all the members of the group have so embraced their Lord they have reached the highest moment of community. And furthermore, they have ideally satisfied their spiritual hunger. This does not mean the end. The work of forming community must always go on. Our spiritual hunger cannot be satisfied at one breaking of the bread.

MEANING IN OUR LIVES THROUGH THE
EUCHARIST

The reason is partly that, as we mature and grow, new possibilities of community and satisfaction emerge. There are some who cannot abide such a community. Jesus challenged His listeners to take the risk and follow Him. As John tells the story, only the apostles remained. Even then Judas is singled out as a man who in the long run saw no real meaning in the teaching and hope that Jesus offered. He could not bring himself to believe that Jesus had the answer to the meaning of life and happiness.

Much is said today about the loss of beauty, the crisis of meaning, and the lonely crowd. Song after song speaks of the hunger for love. The gospel account of the bread of life is an attempt to show how Jesus speaks to these problems.

The first loaves miracle took place in the beauty by the lake. Jesus worked through conversation, teaching, and personal risk to draw the people together, to rescue them from their loneliness. Now in the sacrament of the Eucharist He does the same. Millions have known the peace of the sacred table. He offers this peace to you too.

CHRIST BRINGS MEANING TO OUR LIVES

Jesus Is the Light of the World

People who are in the public eye are always anxious about their image: they want the public to know them, and think of them in the best possible light. So long as they seek to project a true and genuine image of themselves this can be helpful, for it is important that the great mass of people get to know as well as possible their public figures.

THE FEAST OF TABERNACLES

Jesus also worked to project an image of Himself that would catch the attention and personal commitment of the world around Him. The sixth and seventh chapters of Saint John's Gospel recall Jesus describing Himself as a pillar of fire and as the living water. These descriptions are set in the context of the Feast of Tabernacles.

Tabernacles was the most popular Jewish feast, though not the most important in the liturgical calendar. In many ways it may be compared to our Christmas celebrations with its lights and songs and general good feeling. Before it became a liturgical event it was simply a farmers' celebration, a harvest festival.

Gradually it began to assume religious meanings. It was convenient for the harvesters to live in temporary huts in the fields during the gathering time. This was reminiscent of the years that Israel lived in tents in the desert, where God Himself was enshrined in a tentlike tabernacle. The words "tent" and "tabernacle" are really the same thing.

The passing years have glamorized the Israelites' desert experience to the point where they felt it had been the ideal existence (*see* page 66). When they were a pilgrim people, they were a pure people, a real Church. The Hebrew name for their desert community was *qahal*. This name implied that they were not merely an organization nor a motley group that happened to be together. Rather, they were a community summoned into existence by God and molded into His witness by His power and presence. God's presence was powerfully symbolized by the image of the pillar of fire.

THE WATER CEREMONY

There were two ceremonies during the Feast of Tabernacles that highlighted the sacred and secular aspects of the event. The first was the procession to the pool of Siloam for the water ceremony. The second was the dazzling dance of the torches that dramatized the fire pillar of the days of the exodus (*see* page 63).

Anyone who knows farmers is aware of how concerned they are about rain. If there is no rain, there won't be any harvest. The water ceremony of the Feast of Tabernacles had a certain rain-making quality about it. Water was carried in procession from the pool of Siloam up to the temple where it was poured out over the altar. God was thanked for the water that brought about the harvests, and begged to send water again for future harvests. Texts from the book of Exodus were read that recalled how God had Moses miraculously bring forth water from the rocks of the desert.

Here was a neat intermingling of secular desires and religious faith. The Israelites needed rain to make their crops grow. Their faith easily associated the work of God as part of this growth process. They were keenly aware of the presence of God in all their human efforts.

CHRIST DESCRIBED HIMSELF AS THE LIVING WATER

It is in the context of this water ceremony that Jesus identified Himself as the living water. Thirsty men should come to Him and drink and He would satisfy them. He was the living rain for the parched earth of hard hearts. Less poetically, this could be understood as Jesus giving men the courage to make correct moral decisions. It really is not too farfetched to introduce the moral dimension here, because the Feast of Tabernacles had many overtones of the celebration of the ten commandments.

The Feast of Tabernacles, therefore, did include a summons for greater fidelity to the law of God and the need for correct moral behavior. The desert days were lived out in the shadow of Sinai where the law was given. It's true that ultimately the Feast of Pentecost became the official celebration of the ten commandments, but Tabernacles never lost its memory of the great Sinai event, when God gave the ten commandments. (*see* page 71).

Jesus still tells men who thirst for moral conviction that they can find courage in Him. Young people whose hearts are dried out, who seem to have no nerve left to face the moral dilemmas of our time, are invited to put their faith in the immediate personal presence of Jesus and thus absorb the impact of the "rain" of His conviction and power.

THE FIRE CEREMONY

The fire ceremony was the second ceremony of the Feast of Tabernacles. The dance of the torches and the lighting of huge candles and lamps recalled the pillar of fire in the desert. The exodus story describes God as a column of fire walking before the people who dwell in darkness (*see* page 63). He leads them

JESUS IS THE LIGHT OF THE WORLD *drawing us out of the darkness of selfishness and prejudice and showing us the true meaning of our lives*

through the darkness to the promised land. He takes them out of confusion and the wasteland into the territory of order and fertility.

Jesus uses this context of the fire to declare that He is the real light of the world. He is indeed the pillar of fire intent on bringing meaning to the lives of men. Because He has acquired a knowledge of the fullest meaning of life, He is able to communicate this to others with an authority that makes life worthwhile.

THE LIGHT OF THE WORLD

It may be that for many young people the complexity of modern life causes them endless confusion. Self-understanding can become increasingly difficult in a world where a thousand conflicting ideals appear on every television screen and in every magazine advertisement. Well, where is the real ideal? Is the problem of finding meaning in life really solved by a good deodorant, a better mouthwash, a faster car or a wilder dance? Are tighter pants or shorter skirts the best clues to the meaning of life?

Jesus claims that His self-understanding is so adequate that He can really be the light of the world. You may be put off by Jesus calling Himself living water and the pillar of fire. You may find such biblical language quaint, and therefore without meaning to a world where water is generally no problem, and the only pillars of fire are those caused by guns used in wars around the world.

It is sometimes hard to keep in mind the mystery that Jesus is a real man as well as truly God (*see* page 201). He had to struggle to develop moral conviction and genuine self-understanding, just as other men do. He was faced with moral choices as described in the temptation in the desert and the agony in the garden. He had to arrive at an understanding of the meaning of His life and the meaning of His mission to the world.

Christ's grasp of personal meaning did not spring forth without effort and thought. What we admire is that He did this so magnificently that no one has ever matched it. There is no arrogance in His saying He is the light of the world. It is the honest and remarkable truth. We have sometimes so idealized Him that we have failed to keep His humanness in mind. We have received the finished product and forgotten Jesus' tears, depression, and strain that went into His discovering the meaning of His existence.

We forget actually how much He was really like us. He should not appear to us as an "answer man." We shouldn't forget that Jesus worked hard for His solutions, just as we must. But Jesus, as a pillar of fire, leads us through our own darkness that we may find, as He did, the meaning of our own lives. This is the hope that lies ahead for all of us.

A MAN OF SIMPLE FAITH
Cure of the Man Born Blind

Physical blindness often serves well as an image of mental and spiritual stubbornness. It is easy enough to feel sorry for someone who is truly blind. But it is extremely frustrating to try to put a point across to someone who refuses to be open to a new idea. Teachers know this frustration when they have to deal with a closed mind. Business executives know it when they vainly try to change a company policy that is ruinous. Some cardinals and bishops at the Second Vatican Council experienced it as they tried to guide the Church into the twentieth century. Such blindness in the area of religion is the stuff that causes prophets to be stoned and angels to weep.

THE SIMPLE BLIND MAN AND THE LEARNED THEOLOGIANS

The ninth chapter of John's Gospel has the long story of the cure of the man born blind. Of course, John intends to get much more across than a mere cure of a local beggar, marvelous as this may be. John sets up a sort of debate between the simple blind man and the learned theologians.

Through a clever use of balanced scenes, John creates a rising peak of testimony in which the "ignorant" blind man verbally raps the knuckles of the clever religious teachers. Ultimately, the blind man becomes the very judge of those who accused him and thought of themselves as his judges. It is a case of he who "does not know" becoming the instructor and judge of those "who do know."

The scene is a crowded street in Jerusalem during the Feast of Tabernacles. Jesus had just claimed that He is the pillar of fire, the light of the world, and now He is going to demonstrate it by bringing total light to a well-known blind beggar (see page 241). The apostles see the beggar and make a typical pious statement about the relation between the supposed sin of this man and his blindness. Or was it his parents who were the sinners?

TOO MUCH TALK AND NOT ENOUGH ACTION

Jesus has no patience with mere religious quibbling to mask unbelief. He is tired of the endless, learned conversations about the poor which kept people so busy talking that they never got around to doing something about the problem. Jesus sees a *man*, not a *moral problem*. This is no time for lofty moralizing. Meaning and hope must be brought to a man who sits humbly on the bare edge of existence. The man, after all, is blind. He needs vision, both to see flowers in spring and to have hope in solving the final meaning of life.

Jesus sends the blind man to the holy pool of Siloam. There he will gain physical sight and raise his eyes to Mount Zion, where the glory of God rests in the temple. Locked within this blind man is a faith that groped through the darkness for the meaning of life, and responds, so hopefully, to God's call.

THE PHARISEES QUESTION AND THREATEN

After the blind man's cure comes questioning. The neighbors are astonished, and question him closely about how his cure

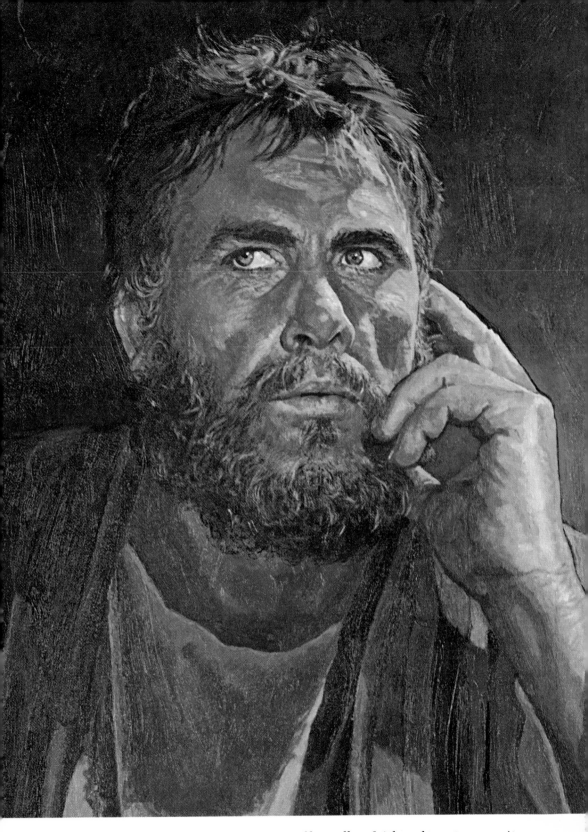

SIMON PETER *was a man of boundless faith and great generosity of heart, qualities that prompted Jesus to make him leader of the apostles*

happened. He is then brought to the Pharisees who are dismayed when the blind man, in his simple wisdom, unhesitatingly declares: "He [Jesus] is a prophet" (John 9:17).

Then his parents are brought in for questioning by the Pharisees. These religious leaders threaten the poor couple that if they are not telling the truth, they will be excommunicated from the Church. If this happens, the parents will be disgraced, shamed before their neighbors and friends, and deprived of whatever little consolation they received from singing the hymns and hearing the sermons. In their old age, they will be robbed of the experience of being in the very presence of the "glory." Consequently, the parents refuse any responsibility for their adult son. They point out that he is a man now and must speak for himself.

THE BLIND MAN ANSWERS THE PHARISEES

By this time, the theologians are pictured as desperate men who must corner their victim at all costs. They pursue the absurd line of argument that Jesus must be a sinner for showing such human concern. The cured man is not one bit ruffled and counters, quite logically, that Jesus, far from being a sinner, is like the prophets of old. He shifts the conversation so that now he is the one asking the questions.

He taunts the Pharisees by remarking that their interest in Jesus is just a bit too intense. If they are so absorbed in such a man, are they planning to become His followers? Is this really just a kind of research project? Is this a method that learned people go through to find out the truth? Are they just trying to prepare themselves for baptism? Do learned people always follow such a difficult path?

THEIR STUDIES HAVE CLOSED THEIR MINDS

This attack has the desired effect of making the Pharisees admit what is really on their minds. They protest their loyalty to Moses and their disdain for Jesus. They are the protectors of the

THE PHARISEES *frequently questioned Jesus about points of law, but He had little patience with this; He preferred to help people with problems rather than talk about the problems*

formal religion and are not easily fooled by any so-called new prophet. They reserve for themselves the right to prophesy, and to anoint a man whom they would consider heir to the mantle of the prophets. They feel, after all, that their long years of religious study have made them professionally competent to recognize the work of God in the world. They can't believe that such an insight could come from a man who hasn't ever read a book.

But the cured man is not impressed. In effect he tells them that, in their case, their studies have closed their minds. All their years of combing the Scriptures, analyzing the words, and talking about the laws have not given them insight, but blurred their vision.

They, who should have been the light of the people are, instead, blind guides. Their theology, which was meant to be a fire that illumined their minds and warmed their hearts, hardened their hearts instead.

THE LEARNED MAN MUST GUARD AGAINST PRIDE

This story is not meant to be an attack on the intellectual life or religious studies. It is, however, meant to draw our attention to the dangers of religious studies that mask unbelief and obstruct others' belief. The simplicity of the cured blind man drives the learned Pharisees into a rage: "You were born in utter sin, and would you teach us?" (John 9:34). And they excommunicated him.

Now it is Jesus who comes seeking this simple man. Jesus crowns the hope of the man who was blind by introducing him to the final meaning of life—belief in the Son of Man. Jesus asks the man to trust that the hope of all mankind is found in Him. He invites the blind man to believe in Him as the final solution to the problem of love. And the man who could have passed no great theology exams kneels before Jesus, and says, simply: "Lord, I believe" (John 9:38).

This story is a warning to every Christian who is proud of his grasp of religion to the point where he is certain that he "sees." It is a reminder that arrogance is the fatal fault of those who trust too much in their religious learning. It is a tale that tempers the proud and calls for a celebration of the most truly Christian man, who is always a *humble man*.

WE MUST LEARN HOW TO TALK TO EACH OTHER

The Good Shepherd and His Flock

We may not know much about shepherds today, but we do know plenty about authority. There is a crisis of authority across the board in our culture. Many families reel under the rebellious attitude of young people. Police often have trouble making arrests because they are not backed up by even normal public support. The traditional suspicion of politicians has grown to the point where millions don't believe what they say any more. Some liberals in the Church cry for freedom of conscience to the extent that they seem to be calling for an unconditional surrender of authority.

THERE HAS ALWAYS BEEN TROUBLE IN THE CHURCH

The shepherds of the Church are under fire today. Every other day bishops are being challenged by some priests and laymen for doing this or not doing that. Just about every week, we hear another story of a priest marrying or a theologian challenging an age-old doctrine of the Church. New "leftwing" magazines tell us that Pope John would be saddened over the failure of his followers to carry out the decrees of the Second Vatican Council. The "new morality" seems to urge everyone to live according to his conscience, with little regard for laws and the decrees of authority.

Trouble is nothing new in the Church. Saint Paul spoke of factions and cliques that threatened to dissolve the infant Church. The Arian rebellion of the fourth century nearly wrecked the Church completely. The Greek schism of the eleventh century left a centuries-old scar of division in the Church. The Protestant Reformation of the sixteenth century splintered the Church into hundreds of competing and jealous sects.

Quite often these revolts and reformations centered their complaints on authority. They raised the problem of the shepherd — the symbol of authority. Jesus, too, addressed Himself to this question. The tenth chapter of John's Gospel records Christ's thoughts about the meaning of a true shepherd. His reflections make more sense when read against the background of a sermon on shepherds given by Ezekiel, in chapter 34 of his book.

EZEKIEL'S DESCRIPTION OF A GOOD SHEPHERD

Ezekiel says that a shepherd should *feed the people, not eat them.* "Ho, shepherds of Israel who have been feeding yourselves! Should not shepherds feed the sheep? You eat the fat, you clothe yourselves with the wool . . . but you do not feed the sheep" (Ezekiel 34:2,3). By feeding, Ezekiel means showing warm, human concern for people: "The weak you have not strengthened, the sick you have not healed, the crippled you have not bound up . . . the lost you have not sought, and with force and harshness you have ruled them" (Ezekiel 34:4).

Ezekiel stresses two aspects of a good shepherd: he should have compassion for those in his congregation, and he should have the energy to search out the ones missing from his community. The good shepherd must walk abroad and discover those who need his

JESUS THE GOOD SHEPHERD *talking to His disciples. Jesus taught that a good shepherd must know His people and must be ready to die for them. Knowing demands communication, and dying requires an extraordinary degree of dedication*

care. He is not to wait for the lost ones to come to his door and ring the bell. He must take the initiative to find them.

Jesus adds two more lines of thought to the plan of Ezekiel. The good shepherd should *know his people* and be willing to *die for them*. "I am the good shepherd; I know my own and my own know me, as the Father knows me and I know the Father; and I lay down my life for the sheep" (John 10:14–15). A good shepherd makes an effort to know his people. He has an interest in their joys and sorrows, their achievements and troubles. He is open enough with them so that they can honestly admit they know him, too. He is not too proud to reveal his humanity, nor so withdrawn as to be a mystery man.

KNOWING DEMANDS COMMUNICATION
AND DYING DEMANDS DEDICATION

When both shepherd and congregation are aware of each other's convictions and feelings, there is a basis of love and a necessity for real community. Such knowledge is deeper than merely knowing people's names. It is more fundamental than simply listening to conversation. It imitates the listening of God whose ear is next to the heart.

The good shepherd is willing to die for his flock. The true pastor is willing to use his energies for the sake of the growth of his people. He is conscious that the use of his strength is an expected and normal part of his dedication to his people. He will not rule them with force and harshness. He will not eat them, living off them like a parasite. Rather, he will work to be a minister to the total person.

Knowing and dying are the special points about shepherds that Jesus emphasizes. *Knowing demands communication, and dying requires an extraordinary degree of dedication.* When there isn't even a "hot line" available between flock and shepherd, then there is a crisis of authority and obedience. When there is a noticeable cooling of self-consecration on the part of the shepherd, then the flock faces a crisis of confidence.

JESUS' DESCRIPTION OF FALSE SHEPHERDS

False shepherds can wreck the Church. Jesus calls them thieves whose only work is to steal and kill and destroy. Being basically indifferent to the true problems of people, they flee when the wolves of confusion attack their flock. At rock bottom, they have really ceased to care for the people.

However, the solution to false shepherds is not found in wild disobedience or name-calling. We live in a world that has come of age. This means that the people are not merely passive sheep, but maturing Christians. In their power is the ability to heal division. If there is a crisis of authority today, it is not because the authorities are a clique of clever exploiters interested only in self gain.

We are not faced, today, with the heartless leadership of Ezekiel's sermon, but with a radical and all too rapid change in the culture. In our new world, relationships have changed so profoundly that there is an obedience gap caused by the slow pace of adjustment. It is what sociologists call a "cultural lag." It is something like a stubborn pole-vaulter insisting on using a bamboo stick instead of a modern fiberglass pole. It is like using a horse instead of a jet plane.

JESUS IS REJECTED *by the leaders of the synagogue at Nazareth. The good shepherd fearlessly speaks the truth and is willing to be denounced and rejected for doing so*

RESTORING THE BALANCE BETWEEN
AUTHORITY AND OBEDIENCE

The tragedy of the present crisis is that there are well-meaning men on both sides of the divide. The parents who are tongue-tied in the face of their teenagers are not simply disinterested, pleasure-seeking adults. No more than teenagers are flighty pleasure-seekers. Rather, there is a credibility gap, seemingly caused by both sides being unable to communicate with each other.

To restore the balance, there must be an agonizing review of the ways in which we communicate with each other. Name-calling and indifference are not solutions. Mature people always search for new gestures of reconciliation. There must be the growing conviction, on both sides, that there is, indeed, much hope for a new and fruitful cooperation.

The psychological need of young people to break the parental apron strings must not be exaggerated into a riotous storming of the castle. There is a point of protesting too much. Authority need not retreat, thinking that every move is a move against it. Knowing and dying on both sides will create a new world that is a Christian celebration of the delicate balance between the shepherds and the sheep.

THROUGH CHRIST WE SURVIVE DEATH
The Raising of Lazarus

Efforts are always being made to penetrate the barrier that prevents communication between this life and the next. Fake spiritualists dupe wealthy old ladies into thinking they are actually talking again with "dear old Harry," but there is little evidence to support the claim. The Church has retained a skepticism about the visions of pious people, only rarely giving her blessing.

The remarkable thing about the Lazarus story, in Saint John's Gospel, is that Lazarus doesn't return from the grave as a scary ghost, but as a full bodied man. And what is even more astonishing is that he doesn't speak of the life beyond the grave. The biblical account shows no interest in the trip that Lazarus took, of the sights and sounds of his journey into the realm of death.

THREE PARTS TO THE STORY

It might be fair to conclude that either the journey into the next life was not a real question for the people of that time, or else Lazarus was unable to tell them anything anyway. The biblical story is less interested in the haunts of the dead than in the hopes of the living. What is important about Lazarus is not the dark corridor of death, but the vision of eternal life which his story promises. The atmosphere of the morgue gives way to the joyous promise of life.

The story is divided into three parts: the *prelude;* the *dialogue;* the *miracle*. The prelude introduces the problem, namely, the critical illness of Lazarus. The dialogue illustrates the meaning of the miracle that is to occur. The miracle is another sign of God summoning men to make the decision of faith.

In the *prelude* Jesus and the apostles have gone into seclusion at a hideaway on the east side of the Jordan, not far from where John the Baptist held his evangelical crusades. Messengers bring news of the quickly failing health of His close friend, Lazarus. As happens so often in John's Gospel, Jesus is presented with a dilemma—and He appears strangely indifferent to it. At Cana, He doesn't seem to share His mother's concern about the empty wine jugs. At the lakeside, He doesn't seem alarmed by the food shortage. He wants to discuss the theology of signs and wonders with the nobleman whose son is dying.

JESUS WANTS HIS AUDIENCE TO THINK

You must not think that this means that Jesus is indifferent to human problems or, on the other hand, that He is like a gambler who delights in knowing that he has the winning ace in his hand. The "delay stories" are meant to show that Jesus wanted to help His audience understand the divine aspect of the problem that lay before them. He is inviting them to join Him in a serious religious reflection on the matter at hand. Plainly, He is asking them to *think*.

He wants them to share with Him the agony and struggle necessary to prepare for the divine breakthrough. He is attempting to drive the magical elements out of faith, to nudge them to understand that faith is not a childish hope for a supernatural trick, but the mature obedience of men open to the great power of God.

He wants to remove faith from the realm of mere heavenly mechanics and situate it on the ground of groping hope and trust. When Jesus feels they have begun to sense the drama of the faith need, He gives the instruction: "Lazarus is dead; and for your sake I am glad that I was not there, so that *you may believe*. But let us go to him" (John 11:14–15).

JESUS BRINGS FREEDOM FROM DEATH

In His *dialogue* with the grief-stricken sisters of Lazarus, Martha and Mary, Jesus strives to explain the meaning of resurrection. They both tell Him that their brother would not have died had He been there. He assures them that their brother will rise again. They are not very impressed with His answer because they think He is referring to the religious belief that all faithful Jews will rise on the last day. This article of faith is of little comfort to them, who want a live brother now rather than in the obscure future. To them, Christ's reply is a sort of theological buck-passing.

This sets the stage for the beauty of Christ's response. He did not have in mind the theory of final resurrection. His daring promise is that, for obedient men, there is the assurance of real life right now. Their brother will rise today. "I am the resurrection and the life; he who believes in me, though he die, yet shall he live, and whoever lives and believes in me shall never die" (John 11:25–26).

Far from avoiding the problem, Jesus addresses Himself to it immediately. He is teaching the two women—and all of us—that He is bringing us freedom from death. He is making the most extravagant claim that Christianity will proclaim through the ages. He is not excluding the possibility of physical death. He is saying rather that this dark hour is not so dark after all. He is calling all men to trust that in Him everyone can survive death and enter into everlasting life.

This is why we can *really live* now. At death life is changed, not taken away. Freedom from death means liberation from the

CHRIST RAISED LAZARUS FROM THE DEAD *to teach us that we should have faith in His promise that we can survive death and enter into everlasting life*

fear that death is the end of everything. Freedom from death implies that we now can attend to the responsibilities of living because we have the glorious promise of living on in Christ Jesus.

The key words in this hope of freedom from death are "responsible living." Wrong attitudes toward death result in either a reckless wasting of life, or a neurotic, convulsive hold on life. Jesus wants to free us from such extreme reactions. The resurrection relieves us of the worry about the afterlife so that we can pay attention to the needs of this life. Naturally, the burden of death and some of its darkness endure, but Christ's promise makes such a burden light.

SUFFERING AND SADNESS REMAIN

In the *miracle*, seldom has the humanity of God shone forth so convincingly as it does when Jesus weeps before the tomb of Lazarus. In His talk with the sisters, He makes clear that, even when a person has faith, he must still face the suffering and sadness of human life. The vision of faith that Christ brings to men cannot erase the burdens of human life. Expertly, that is shown to us in this story.

The event ends with Jesus confidently calling forth Lazarus from the grave. Here is an ultimate breakthrough of God's power in history and the confirmation of the promise of life after death.

As you can see, the issues in the Lazarus story are not a superficial report of "life on the other side," but rather a forceful declaration that there is life in the beyond. This incident is a page in the story of freedom which Jesus brings us. In this case, the freedom from death is explained. Here is a religious statement of deep meaning for all those who wish to live this life to the fullest as responsible and mature Christians.

JESUS REVEALED HIMSELF BY WORD AND DEED

Christ's Aim Is to Change People

It is common enough for people to want to see great men. Tourists jam Saint Peter's square to see the pope. Travelers shuffle by the gates of Buckingham Palace hoping to get a glimpse of royalty. Well-known politicians know the value of personal exposure to raise their popularity ratings. The film and pop music public relations men make sure that fan clubs grow up around the stars. Autographing pictures is a normal detail for famous people.

HOW DID JESUS REVEAL HIMSELF TO THE WORLD?

The coming of Jesus, however, is not a subject for the phony gimmickry often used today to bring people to the attention of the public. Christ deliberately avoided noisy fan clubs. He wants no artificial popularity. He revealed Himself in such a quiet, restrained manner that it would rattle the nerves of public relations men.

There are two passages in the Bible that characterize the way Jesus revealed Himself to the world: Isaiah 60 and John 1:1–18. We shall devote ourselves mainly to John's text, referring later to the song of Isaiah. The quotation from John speaks of Christ's

STEPHEN WAS MARTYRED *for fearlessly proclaiming Christ's message. Christ's aim was to change people, but people are not easily changed. Christians will always suffer when they courageously follow their Master's example*

image in terms of *Logos* or Word. The most general way of making ourselves known to one another is by means of speech. God's revelation to us, in a sense, is a *happening in words* rather than actions. For many years, it was thought that John used the *Logos-*Word idea because it appealed to the Greeks, who thought of a *"logos"* as an important principle in the creation of the world.

More recent thinking, however, suggests that John could just as well have been using Hebrew thinking. The Hebrew term for word is *dabar*. This also happens to mean "deed," namely, the word acted out. Hence, there is a close connection between word and deed. The theme of *dabar*-word is quite common in the Old Testament.

JESUS IS THE CREATIVE WORD

The book of Genesis meditates on the *creative* word. God said, "Let there be light," and there was light. Jesus used the creative word. He said to a cripple, "Get up and walk," and the lame man walked. Jesus took bread, offered it to His apostles in the upper room and said, "This is my body." And it became His body. Peter sent the creative word of God out over the square at Pentecost, and from those present came a new creation of three thousand Christians. Jesus not only speaks this creative word. He *is* the Word. As He told us, He does not just teach the truth. *He is the truth.*

The word of God is also *dynamic.* Being dynamic does not mean shouting like a cheerleader, or sweating like a golf pro, or being a nervous wreck over religion. The dynamism of God's word means that it has within itself the power to change the person who hears it. The old proverb says, "Seeing is believing." Saint Paul claims that faith comes from *hearing.* When the word of God is properly heard and proclaimed it has the power to change the listener.

CHRISTIANS MUST CHANGE THE WORLD, NOT BORE IT TO DEATH

Repentance implies a deep interior change. Read chapter 10 of Matthew's Gospel where Jesus gives some advice to missionaries. "As you enter the house, salute it. And if the house is worthy, let your peace come upon it" (Matthew 10:12–13). The whole chapter emphasizes the dynamism of Christ's message. He is out to change people. "Do not think I have come to bring peace on earth; I have not come to bring peace, but a sword" (Matthew 10:34).

Christians who present a message that is so weak and almost boring that it is not even challenged by anyone are not faithful to the dynamic word. The Bible cannot be just a dusty document, quaint with age. It commands us now to shed our light before men. As the Negro spiritual put it, "Let your little light shine." A real Christian reveals Christ. This happens best in charity. Never in the Church is Christ more clearly shown to the world than in that mysterious and delightful moment when you meet an expression of genuine Christian charity.

WHAT IS THE "END-TIME"?

The word of God, which can change the world, pushes us toward the final stage in the transformation of that world. We in the Church are already living in the "end-time" which is the final age of the world. It is the age when God's power is being fully revealed to men. We live now in the last age of man's relationship to God.

The end-time is described in the book of Revelation (Apocalypse) in terms of four horsemen. A white horse of victory is quickly introduced, to be seen again later. A red horse rides into history. The rider is to take away peace from the earth. He is a sign of war. Next arrives the black horse of famine and hunger. The rider cries out: "A quart of wheat for a denarius, and three quarts of barley for a denarius" (Revelation 6:6). Then comes the pale horse whose rider's name is death.

These unholy three are commissioned to dominate part of the earth, killing with the sword, famine, and plague. Our own age has seen these grim riders. The violent death of sixty million people in the wars of this century is a painful reminder of the pale horse of death and the red horse of war. Throughout the world thousands die of hunger every day, and scientists forecast dreadful famines for the next decade. The black horse of famine will ride.

WHO RIDES THE WHITE HORSE?

Amid all this gloom there is a fourth rider who brings hope. "Then I saw heaven opened, and behold a white horse! He who

PETER *said to Jesus: "You have the message of eternal life, and we believe, we know you are the Holy One of God"*

sat upon it is called Faithful and True, and in righteousness he judges and makes war. His eyes are like a flame of fire. . . . He is clad in a robe dipped in blood, and the name by which he is called is The *Word* of God" (Revelation 19:11–13).

The rider on the white horse is the sign of hope in the midst of hunger and death. His name is the Word of God. He speaks a vision which promises that ultimately the human dilemma will be solved. He speaks of light to a dark world, peace to the hating, and a banquet table for the hungry.

We have seen the theme of the *word* in the Bible in terms of its creativity, its dynamism, and its special presence in the end-time. The *Logos*-Word of John grows out of such thinking. Jesus is the creative Word ruling over the continuing development of the world and urging it toward progress that makes men free and able to live as human beings.

JESUS IS WHERE THE ACTION IS

Jesus is the dynamic Word, not as One who lived long ago, but as the message arriving in our own time, changing us and calling us to responsibility for the care of the earth. He is, in a sense, where the action is, calling us to aid the inner city, assist the underdeveloped nations, and work for the dignity of all men.

Jesus is the last Word, alive today as the One who works to keep men realizing there is hope, and that the final meaning of life is found in God. He wants the world to realize that the ultimate answer to human doubts and questions is not really completely found within the world. We must also consider *the beyond* in our midst.

The *Logos* section of John ends by saying Jesus is the "glory" who has pitched His tent among us. He is full of faithfulness and openness to us. It is here that we can turn to the old, joyful words of Isaiah which are read every Epiphany:

"Arise, shine; for your light has come
and the glory of the Lord has risen upon you"
(Isaiah 60:1).

THE KIND OF LOVE CHRIST TAUGHT
The Sermon on the Mount

To hope that the love taught by Christ is the final solution to the problem of love in the world seems to be dreaming the impossible dream. There are other forms of love competing with the one Jesus promoted. The love of self is one kind. Love in terms of getting a return is another form. Self-love and "return love" are good as long as there is no exaggeration.

THE IMPORTANCE OF LOVING YOURSELF

It is important to love yourself. This is another way of saying that you should have a healthy acceptance of who you are. This means you have an honest appreciation of your talents. You do not underestimate yourself; nor are you overly idealistic about your possibilities. Love of self becomes selfishness when you force others to serve your self-image. You interfere with others' rights when you use others to acquire an exaggerated sense of importance about your personal dignity and felt needs. This is the wrong kind of self-love.

"RETURN LOVE"

Love for the sake of a return, the second type of love mentioned, plays a part in your personal development. This love enchants the mind as you reach out to know others. It makes you morally sensitive as you awaken to the shining goodness of others. It sharpens your powers of judgment as it brings you to dwell on the likenesses and differences between yourself and others.

This love makes it possible for you to appreciate the meaning and value of affection. You can know what it means to have someone constantly thinking about you, even as you are absorbed in your concern for them. It is when this happens that girls "could have danced all night," and guys find it hard to stay away from "the street where she lives."

These are some of the values of "return love." But, this kind of love, too, can be spoiled. You can ruin this love by turning it into a bargaining session or putting it on a cash basis: this much love for that much love. Start measuring the transaction of love and you have made it a charade. Enter your love deeds into a ledger, and your debits and credits will add up to a grand total of disillusionment.

A THIRD KIND OF LOVE

Jesus proposes a third form of love. The New Testament name for it is *agape* (pronounced ah-*ga*-pay). This is love that is given even when there is no return. This love does not exclude proper self-love, nor does it frown on "return love."

One of the best explanations of *agape* is the Sermon on the Mount. (*See* Matthew, chapters 5 through 7.) Unfortunately, the Sermon on the Mount is often called the law of Christ. The statement is true. It is the interpretation that misses the point. The *law* of Christ becomes the *laws* of Christ. The numerous bits and pieces of the Sermon seem to become rules and laws. Nothing could be further from the truth. *What Jesus is talking about is love, not laws.* The key is found in the opening lines of the Ser-

THE SERMON ON THE MOUNT *is a masterly summary of Christ's teaching, and introduces the new Age He has come to establish. The Old Law will not be destroyed but fulfilled in the New, whose motivation is love, not fear*

mon where you read the eight beatitudes. The beatitudes are eight
different ways of describing the profound love that can exist between God and an honest man. The Bible often uses the word
"covenant" to picture such love.

WHAT KIND OF LOVE IS THIS?

In the beatitudes, Jesus is saying that the *agape* – love – He encourages Christians to practice is rooted in the covenant between
men and God. In both the covenant and in *agape,* it is God who
first loves us. The depth of such a relation can make the impossible dream come true. The dream is that *agape* is the final solution to the problem of love in the world. Who is to believe this
promise of Jesus? Can such a love really work? Ask yourself what
would happen if whole nations practiced *agape*? What would happen if every Christian believed it would truly work? It may seem
to be an impossible dream, but it only *seems* impossible. Jesus has
taught us: "It is a possible dream!"

Throughout the rest of His Sermon, Jesus hammers home His
point. Walk the extra mile. Give your second coat. Be as free in
your heart as the birds of the air and the lilies of the field. Love
your enemies. Bless those who persecute you. Break the circle of
revenge. Don't parade your good deeds. Don't pray as hypocrites
do. Fast in secret. Serve only one master. Be the salt of the earth,
the light of the world, the tree that bears good fruit.

EVERY MAN CAN HAVE THIS KIND OF LOVE

These are not rules of Christ so much as they are images which
describe the *quality* of the love He wants you to have. He wants
you to be Christians of the second mile, that is, He wants you to
let your love be as tireless as His love is. Jesus is fully aware that
love becomes especially dreary when it sees no return. Who wants
to make an investment that has no dividends? Who wants to keep
the store open when nobody comes to buy?

Jesus claims that this is one investment that works even when it seems to fail. The time when it seems to be failing is what we call the way of the cross. There is a dark and tangled road for *agape*. You know the attractive side of love—the moonlight and roses and tenderness. This is the happy time of dances, varsity letters, and the best-looking date in town.

Jesus has no quarrel with the beauty of love. He can celebrate it as quickly as anyone else. He honored the young lovers at Cana with a miracle of wine. He gave His hand and pledge of friendship to His apostles at the Last Supper. What is unique about Christ's teaching on love is that He promises a way to make the beauty of love the common experience of every man in the world. This can be achieved only by *agape*, and *agape* demands that we cope with the tragic side of love. This suffering is nothing less than the pain of the cross. Jesus assures us that this love—*agape*—is the highest and noblest form of love.

THE CHRISTIAN TASK: PRACTICE THIS LOVE

The Christian task is to practice *agape*. The real faith of the Christian community is the trust that the love spoken of by Jesus in the Sermon on the Mount is the real solution to the problem of love in the world. Perhaps this will appear unbelievable to some. And others may reject it as an absurdity. Some again will ignore it as a childish ideal, and practical men may shake their heads and say it simply won't work. But, every so often, someone will catch fire and bear the flame of this love. It is contagious. Saint Francis of Assisi caught it and sang about it on the roads of Europe. Pope John caught it and stirred the imagination of the world. *What about you?*

MIRACLES
Signs of God's Presence

People still talk of miracles today. At the World's Fair in Montreal, Canada, Expo '67, there was a pavilion that showed movies with the title, "Miracles of Science." A million people every year journey to Lourdes either hoping for a miraculous cure or to reverence the place where such cures occurred. Men walk on the moon; pharmacies sell miracle drugs; and research centers promise even greater signs and wonders.

TODAY THE WORLD TALKS OF MAN'S MIRACLES

Has it occurred to you that, in our so-called scientific age, many persons cast doubt on the miracles of religion, then use the idea of miracles for man-made wonders? To paraphrase the "Ancient Mariner": *Miracles, miracles everywhere — and not a drop of faith.* The word "miracle" formerly meant a special sign of God's presence. Today, it is used almost exclusively to praise human cleverness.

All this is not to say that men should not gratefully praise the tough-minded achievements of science. But we should regret the scorn sometimes heaped on religious claims to miracles. And we should be appalled by those who deny that Jesus performed the signs and wonders attributed to Him in the Gospels. Finally, let's be aware that modern man fails to see any religious meaning in the wondrous productions of our laboratories.

Let us applaud the winners of the Nobel Prize, but let's shy away from making gods out of our white-coated researchers. It would be a mistake to put our wonder-workers on thrones. Ultimately, it is God to whom the glory should be given.

THE TEN MIRACLES IN MATTHEW'S GOSPEL

This may become clearer to us, if we first take a closer look at the miracle stories in the Gospels. In Saint Matthew's Gospel, chapters 8–10, we find an account of ten miracles of Jesus, followed by an explanation of the role of these wonders in the apostolate.

It will be easier to appreciate Matthew's point if we remember the general presentation he had in mind. He wanted to portray Jesus for his Jewish readers as the greatest person imaginable. Up to this time, no man had greater claim to Jewish esteem than Moses. Hence, Matthew surrounds Jesus with qualities and details that were typical of Moses. This is something like a sports writer speaking of a modern baseball star in terms of stories from the life of Babe Ruth.

It was popular to say that Moses wrote the first five books of the Bible. The common Jewish name for these books was "the law." Moses was called the law-giver. In imitation of this, Matthew divided his Gospel into five parts. In each section, he drew a parallel between Jesus and Moses. He used this technique both to show the greatness of Jesus, and His superiority to Moses.

THE TEN WONDERS OF JESUS
AND THE TEN PLAGUES

In the previous article, we studied the Sermon on the Mount (*see* page 266). There, Saint Matthew presents Jesus as the new law-giver on a new Sinai. Here, in this article about miracles, we shall see that Matthew draws a parallel between the ten wonders of Jesus and the ten plagues instigated by Moses in Egypt (*see* page 60).

The plagues of Egypt were ten signs of God's displeasure with the Pharaoh, who stood as the symbol of the evils of injustice and cruelty. The Egyptian leader had dehumanized the Jews. He robbed them of their rights, their religious heritage, and human dignity. The ten plagues signaled the advance of God against such a kingdom of evil.

We can find the same meaning, only in a richer fashion, in Matthew's account. Jesus cleanses the lepers, thus restoring their human dignity. They need no longer be outcasts of society. Jesus cools the fever of Peter's mother-in-law, raises people from the dead, relieves the embarrassment of the dumb, erases the humiliations of the paralyzed, and eases the torments of the mentally afflicted.

As God once made the Red Sea safe for passage, so now Jesus calms a storm at sea. As Moses, by the power of God drove out the devils of Egypt, so now Jesus drives out the demons that would elude and enslave helpless men. The new pharaoh is the sum total of human ills that frustrate the growth and dignity of men. The new pharaoh is the presence of evil in the world. By evil, I mean the presence of a spirit in the heart of man that refuses to see anything beyong the human. The evil spirit flatters man into denying that there is anything beyond himself, and urges man to forget the presence of the divine in the midst of the world.

GOD IS AT WORK IN THE WORLD

Over and over again, it becomes clear that miracles are signs of the divine presence. They are wonders which prove God's intention to raise man to the peak of human dignity. They are examples of the graciousness of God, and they rescue men from the chaos that comes from forgetting God altogether.

JESUS *stood up in the boat and said "Peace, be still." Immediately the wind ceased and there was a great calm. Jesus then said to His disciples: "Why are you afraid? Have you no faith?" (Mark 4:35–41)*

Miracles are that extra dimension of life that should cause us to stop and take notice. They should stimulate a shock of recognition: man is not alone in the world; God is in our midst. Jesus told His followers that the miracles are a way of saying that the kingdom is at hand. By the kingdom, He meant the Church. By the Church, He meant that, through His community of believers, God is powerfully at work in the world to accomplish the dreams of men. These dreams are peace for the world, the victory of universal love, the establishment of justice, and the promise of hope for every man.

The miracles tell us that the kingdom is always at hand. What we, as the community of believers, must do, is work to make this kingdom a reality for everyone. God has not gone back on His promises. It is the Church which must make these promises available in a practical way. Don't forget that the Church is the community of believers. Don't forget that *we are that Church.*

THE MIRACLE OF LOVE

The kingdom is at hand, but no one will know it if we do not show it. The miracle we must perform is the mighty work of love. To you and me, as to all Christians, is entrusted the miracle of making love a standard of action in the world. Technology is the world's miracle of our time. But love remains the enduring religious miracle of all time. Scientists can make the bomb, but only love can control it. Technicians can make the automobile, but only human concern can keep it safe. Botanists can make new possibilities for millions of tons of wheat. It takes love to make sure the world does not go hungry. We must pledge ourselves to the miracle of love and believe that it will work.

CHRIST DESCRIBED THE CHURCH IN PARABLES
A Community of Faith

Sometimes it is better to describe than to define. A definition has a way of putting an end to a discussion because of the limits that it sets. I have seen some black looks on the faces of young people when they heard adults defining a teenager. Description is a little easier to take because it doesn't close the question. A description is gracious enough to imply that there is something more. A young person is much more than a definition can indicate.

A CHALLENGE TO BE ACCEPTED
OR REJECTED

When Jesus wanted to portray the Church He was founding, He chose to describe it, rather than define it. This is why He used parables. Parables describe, they don't define. Parables have the power of poetry. Poetry, as a descriptive device, always hints that the reality is greater than any one thing you can say about it. The reality of the Church is much greater than any one picture we can give of it.

Scan the thirteenth chapter of Saint Matthew's Gospel and you will find Christ's description of the Church—the famous parables of the kingdom. Here, Jesus presents you with a set of images that attempt to give you a feel for the meaning of the Church. These images are not only things He has to say about the Church, they are also significant points to remember about the kingdom of God. Like the picture of a loved one you may carry in your wallet, the parables of the kingdom give you a loving reminder of the Church.

Each of these parables fills out the broad view of the meaning of the Church. The longest and most famous of these stories is the *parable of the sower*. When the Christian missionary proclaims the kingdom of God, he is like a farmer scattering seed. The farmer knows that some of the seeds will find good ground and grow. Other seeds will meet obstacles and fail to take root.

A good Christian missionary announces the kingdom to all available men. He knows that his missionary work faces both the pleasing prospects of success and the depressing results of failure. Some men will accept the kingdom with joy. Others will consider it an intellectual curiosity. A third group will reject it altogether and, perhaps, even work to frustrate its progress. The missionary presents the Church as a challenge which must either be accepted or rejected. He is so serious about this challenge that he will not let anyone be indifferent, just as the farmer is not indifferent to his hopes for a harvest.

CHRIST WARNED ABOUT EVIL IN THE CHURCH

Jesus tells a second parable about *the wheat and the weeds*. An enemy sows destructive weeds in the field that threaten the vitality of the crop. In this story, Jesus draws our attention to the existence of evil in the life of the Church. Everybody in the kingdom is not a saint. You can fairly well count on a Judas in every congregation. In your enthusiasm for the integrity of the Church, you may want to root out the sinners and the traitors. Because of this, Jesus urges a realistic and healthy caution. "Let both grow to-

JESUS, *by word and example, showed us that in His Church riches and worldly power have no place: the poor and the humble will put the rich and the strong to shame*

gether until the harvest; and at harvest time I will tell the reapers, Gather the weeds first and bind them in bundles to be burned, but gather the wheat into my barn" (Matthew 13:30).

You must not think that Jesus wants you to be indifferent to the evil men in the Church. Rather, He wants you to have the hard-eyed realism to know that such things happen in a sinful world. You may, indeed, work to convert the sinners and soften their harmful influence on the community. But a fanatic campaign to stamp them out may threaten the existence of the good men as well as the bad. Plainly put, a real Church is a human Church. Sinners will live within the community of faith. This is an unpleasant picture, but a true one. It is part of the description of the Church and Jesus tells you so.

THE HUMBLE CAN PUT THE
STRONG TO SHAME

Jesus continues His description with the images of *the mustard seed and the leaven.* The smallest of all seeds grows into the biggest tree. The tiny piece of leaven enlarges the dough into a fine loaf of bread. Here He is saying that the beginnings of the Church are always small. The kingdom is not promoted by sending a huge expeditionary force to land on the beaches of the pagans. Big publicity campaigns, flashy advertising, and strong-arm tactics are not the true way to present the gospel. The weak, that is the truly humble, are to put the strong to shame. If it is the other way around, then we raise a doubt about the honesty of the faith.

The Church is a community of faith. The act of faith must be made in freedom. Massive techniques would be like a bulldozer. Rather than inviting a man to believe from his vantage point of freedom, you might find yourself forcing him to believe, or else you would dazzle him to the point that he would forget to use sound judgment in his decision. No moment is more delicate than that quiet time when a man, in the fullness of his freedom and in humble openness, makes the decision to say "yes" to the call of Christ. We would distort the faith if we attempted to make a man believe, even if we are using what seem like the noblest of tactics. To either trick or force a man into the Church fails to be like the mustard seed or the leaven.

MEMBERSHIP IN CHRIST'S CHURCH MAKES
SERIOUS DEMANDS

The last series of parables is about *the hidden treasure,* the *merchant in search of fine pearls,* and *the sorting of the good and bad fish.* The treasure and pearl stories focus on the candi-

JESUS *said: "If there is one of you who has not sinned, let him be the first to cast a stone at her." Membership in His Church demands that we practice Christlike compassion*

date for the Church. The parable of the fish concerns the role of salvation and judgment in the life of the kingdom.

The candidate for Christianity will be a man of absolute commitment. Once he has discovered the message of Christian love, nothing will hold him back. He will sell all he has to possess this treasure. This means he will be willing to surrender all the values of his former life which are inconsistent with Christ's call to love. He will see that his vision of the possibilities of Christian life will make him a totally new man. The candidates for the Church will be men of the highest idealism.

The separation of the good and bad fish highlights the theme of salvation and judgment in the parables of the kingdom. The Church of Christ is ultimately an either-or affair. The kind of love to which Christ calls us is either practiced or it isn't. Those who embrace this love will be saved. Those who refuse will be judged. "Judged" is a biblical way of saying "damned." We can see the seriousness of Christ's message.

Membership in His Church is not to be taken lightly. It is not to be reduced to the position of a pleasant and casual social club for suburbanites. It should not be the ecclesiastical counterpart of a country club. It is far more important than heading the student council or leading the basketball team. The demand of Jesus is for trust in the power of love. Those who parade under the name of Jesus, yet fail to practice His solution to the problem of love, are unworthy to be the Church. They will be judged, not saved.

Here, then, is the description. The Christian missionary presents the Church as a challenge. Realistically, he knows that evil will affect the community of believers. He will beware of the dangers of allowing the strong to dominate the weak. He will rejoice in the candidate who comes with the highest of ideals. He knows the Church always stands at the crossroads of salvation and judgment. He believes firmly that the work of Jesus marches on.

THE TRAINING CHRIST GAVE TO HIS APOSTLES
His Personal Example

Newspaper reports on the Vietnam war had an interesting story about the capturing of documents that described the training of Viet Cong soldiers. It was surprising how extensive the details of the training were. The documents dealt with the ideals which should inspire the soldiers, the different strategies for guerrilla warfare and mass-army warfare, and the collection of taxes to finance the military.

We are all familiar, by now, with the training techniques used in China for the Red Guard. Armed with the sayings of Mao Tse-tung, they go forward as apostles of radical communism. They faithfully carry the small book of the master's sayings with them everywhere they go.

INSTRUCTION AND PERSONAL EXAMPLE

If the leaders of the Viet Cong and the Red Guard can take the training of their apostles so seriously, it is not surprising that Jesus was equally absorbed in schooling His men for the apostolate. He spent the years of His public life working on the formation of the twelve. The central lesson in this formation was the example of Jesus Himself. The apostles had the privilege of contacting the greatest personality who ever lived. This touch with greatness at so intimate a level was the central feature of their training.

But Jesus also used instruction, as well as His personal example. One of the obvious training examples is in Saint Matthew's Gospel, chapter 10. Here we read that Jesus gave the apostles the power to cast out devils and to heal the sick. In modern terms, He made them concerned with the effects of evil on body and mind. He taught them how to relieve people from the demons that tormented their souls. He instructed them in the powers of healing.

The difference between then and now is that Jesus centered these works on faith. He did not rely exclusively on secular methods. We use the word "exclusively" because we would not want to imply that Jesus did not respect purely secular techniques.

Christian Scientists and faith healers have misread these texts. They have made an unnatural division between faith and medicine. The results have been tragic. Children have died of such ailments as appendicitis because doctors were not allowed to operate. The belief was that faith alone would cure the ailment. What Jesus taught the apostles was that faith and human effort should combine for the healing process.

Almost every Christian family has a story about a "miracle" of healing that was attributed to profound prayer and the faith of the loved ones at the bedside. This does not, in any way, lessen the need and respect for the professional doctor and psychologist. It is just that faith adds a dimension to the mystery of human healing that Jesus does not want us to forget.

HELP FOR THE LOST AND LONELY

Christ's second point in instructing the apostles is that they are to go to the lost sheep of Israel first, telling them the kingdom of heaven is at hand. In modern terms, this would mean going to the lonely and the lost in our society. It does not mean dealing only

JAMES AND JOHN, *the sons of Zebedee, were helping their father mend the nets when Jesus called them. "Immediately they left the boat and their father, and followed Him"* (Matthew 4:21–22)

with Catholics and forgetting non-Catholics. It is a call to bring the joy of the gospel to any rejected person anywhere.

Who are some of the lonely and the lost, today? The teenager who is confused about the meaning of life and the darkness of the future. The rich man who finds that his vast bank account still leaves him empty inside. The Negro who has no hope of ever advancing in society. The despairing poor whites of Appalachia. The bewildered families of war-torn countries. The social outcasts on skid row. The aimless, middle-aged woman in suburbia who has turned to alcohol. The old people who are forced to live on the edge of society. The apostle should go to them with the good news that the kingdom is at hand.

The apostle will not *tell* them of the kingdom first. He will *bring* the kingdom to them by his actions. The apostle will work to bring justice to the Negro, provide meaningful lives for the old, inspire aimless young people. In other words, he will provide help and encouragement for all who are in need. Act now, preach later. When the apostle has given the lonely and the lost an experience of the kingdom, then his words about its presence make more sense.

TRAVELING LIGHT

A third point that Jesus insists on is: travel light. "Take no gold, nor silver, nor copper in your belts, no bag for your journey, nor two tunics, nor sandals, nor a staff. . . ." (Matthew 10:9–10). Travel light! The apostle must have the mobility of a guerrilla fighter. He cannot be weighed down with the concern for large property holdings, extensive investments, and vast possessions. Such things tie him down. They turn him into a caretaker. And, as in the parable of the wedding feast, he might refuse to go to the banquet because he has to take care of his property.

The greatest examples in history of the "travel light" theme are Jesus, Saint Paul, Saint Francis of Assisi. Of course, all the apostles and saints are good illustrations of this. It is just that these

THE APOSTLES *were warned by their Master that when they go forth to preach His gospel they can expect to be persecuted*

three are obvious examples. Saint Francis is the most romantic picture of this theme. He literally gave up his estates so that he could travel light. In giving up all, he gained all. He sang along the highways of Europe as a troubadour for Christ.

EXPECT OPPOSITION

A fourth point that Jesus makes is that His apostles can anticipate opposition and severe criticism. They may even have to die for the cause. After all, the disciple is not above the master. Christ's followers can expect to be stoned like Stephen, imprisoned like Paul, and crucified like Peter. A Christian apostle today may hear the screams of those who oppose his stand on racial justice, experience the stinging rebuke of self-righteous people, and sweep up the glass from the windows broken in his home by hostile neighbors.

THERE IS A RISK INVOLVED
IN STANDING UP FOR A CAUSE

Once you stand up for a cause, you take the risk of knowing opposition. Once you decide to carry out Christ's challenge that there be justice and charity for all, you are open to attack from those who refuse to allow such justice and charity to occur. Even so gentle a man as Pope John suffered many lonely nights because of opposition he experienced from those who did not wish to see the fulfillment of the causes for which he worked.

Jesus realized His apostles would be storm centers. "Do not think that I have come to bring peace on earth; I have not come to bring peace, but a sword" (Matthew 10:34). It is not that Jesus really wishes such division, but He knows full well that justice and charity are only achieved with a struggle. The dark forces of evil must be fought, not sweetly tolerated.

Carry these sayings of Jesus (from Matthew, chapter 10) with you as faithfully as a Red Guard carries the sayings of Mao. Be stronger in following Jesus than the Red Guards are in following Mao. Christ brings the real kingdom of God. It is your privilege to be His apostle.

A CHURCH FOR ALL NATIONS
Concern for People's Problems

In all big cities throughout the world there are ghettoes. The rich and prosperous live in their neat clean houses and have very little or no contact with the poor who exist in their slums. Not only the rich and poor live in their respective worlds. The Church, too, can live in its own ghetto. Jesus faced this problem with Judaism. We face it with our own Church. That is why the Second Vatican Council issued a document on the need for the Church to have dialogue with the world.

PHARISEES WANTED TO MAKE JUDAISM A GHETTO

Christ found some of the Pharisees of His time to be small-minded. They claimed that Judaism was the only true religion. Some of the Pharisees were jealous of their traditions, suspicious of foreigners, and not very interested in making converts. Some of the Pharisees said that Judaism had no foreign mission society, and they were excessively strict with the few who came and asked admission to the religion.

Instead of making Judaism a light to the nations, these Pharisees hid its light under a bushel. Rather than work to make the prophetic dream of justice and peace come true, they cursed the Gentiles, grudgingly compromised with ruling powers, and kept proudly to themselves. They listened to the story of Jonah's successful missionary journey to Nineveh, but did not feel the need to put this teaching into practice.

PARABLES WARN THE CHURCH AGAINST A GHETTO ATTITUDE

Jesus wanted to make sure that His Church would not suffer from the same attitudes. In parable after parable, especially those in Saint Matthew's Gospel, He taught that His was a Church for all nations. Take the story of the laborers in the vineyard, for instance (*see* Matthew 20:1–16). Those laborers who came at the eleventh hour and received the same pay as the first laborers are the Gentiles. They are representatives of every nation under heaven who come to share the good news of Jesus.

In another vineyard tale, Jesus tells the story of the tenants who killed the master's servants and murdered his son (*see* Matthew 21:33–41). The master decided to take the vineyard away from the evil tenants and give it to others. The others are the just men of every land, and the vineyard is the kingdom and the Church. So Jesus, again, teaches that His kingdom will be universal.

Christ picks up this theme once again in the parable of the wedding feast (*see* Matthew 22:2–10). In this lesson, a king invited the usual guests to a banquet in honor of the marriage of his son. They refused to come and insulted the king and beat his servants. Hence, new guests were called in from the streets of the world. These three parables attack three kinds of narrowness in the Church: self-righteousness, the closed mind, and the caretaker mentality.

Self-righteousness is attacked in the story of the laborers who were hired at the eleventh hour. Those laborers who had been

THE GOOD SAMARITAN. *In parable after parable Jesus taught that His was a Church for all nations, a Church that had concern for people's problems*

hired earlier cried out with rage. In effect, they were saying: if you haven't worked for salvation like we did, then you don't deserve it. A statement like this reduces salvation to a purely human effort. It implicitly denies that salvation is due, first of all, to the graciousness of God. Only God can save man. Once man believes he can save himself, he has no need for God. He becomes a god to himself.

A LESSON ON THE CLOSED MIND

The parable of the murderous tenants is a clear lesson on the closed mind. The tenants are the members of the Church. The master is God. The servants are the prophets sent by God to help the people have open minds. The son is Jesus. The tenants do not want to listen to the prophets who tell them about the real meaning of God's work in the world.

The prophets call the tenants to justice, but the tenants are selfish. The prophets urge the people to be a real people of God, demonstrating to all the world what a paradise a godly community could be. But the tenants don't want to listen to this. The prophets want the tenants to forget the power plays of politics and use the way of the humble. But they are only interested in securing the vineyard for themselves. They are a cautious, careful lot, unwilling to be open to the mysterious ways of God.

The master's son tries everything to awaken them, but they are too deaf. They can only rush at him with blind rage and crush him. It is the same today. Many in the Church have closed minds. The "tenants" still balk at the call to social justice; they still love the devious power plays of politics, and the ever-so-safe tried and true ways. They no longer stone and crucify the prophets, but they do make things uncomfortable. The parable teaches that people with closed minds will lose their Church and it will be given to others. We have yet to see how this will work out in our own day.

A CARETAKER CHURCH

The parable of the wedding feast criticizes the caretaker mentality—the attitude of being too busy taking care of *things* to take care of *people*. God summoned the Jews to the exciting work of building a new Church. This was taught in the parable of the wedding feast of the master's son. The invited guests—who represented the Jews—had no time to come; they were too busy caring for farms, cattle purchases, and their own family affairs. This is meant to be an image of Judaism itself. It had become a caretaker Church. The Jews had built an enormous temple that required huge taxes to pay for its upkeep and an army of people to staff its endless functions. Crews of workmen continued to lavish new decorations on its walls. The clergy were arranged into a hierarchy who were so busy with administration that they never really met the people. No time was left for the meaning of life, the deep questions of men or the problem of unbelievers.

There are some who look upon our Church today as having somewhat the same problem. We are being criticized for being a caretaker Church. The Second Vatican Council was a wedding feast that summoned us to carefully look ourselves over and check for flaws and errors. It remains to be seen how well we can shake off our narrow-minded attitudes to see some of the ways in which the Church can become meaningful to the world. God is inviting people from the streets of the world to sit at our banquet table. Are we ready to echo His voice? Can we be strong enough to help the halt and the lame to share the riches of the kingdom? Are you ready to bring the Church to all people?

THE MEANING OF JESUS IS KNOWN ONLY BY FAITH
Christ's Secret Is Love

Secrets almost always have a fascination. The big auto companies hold America in suspense each fall while they keep their models for the new year a deep secret. Pro football teams make the darkest secrets of the plays that they will use to beat the opposition. Popes hold the clergy who expect to be made cardinals in suspense by keeping their names secret to the last minute. Fashion houses take great pains to keep secret their new styles.

WHY DID JESUS WANT HIS SECRET KEPT?

Jesus, too, had a secret, and on a number of occasions warned certain people not to reveal it. Read the following texts:

"And he healed many who were sick with various diseases, and cast out many demons; and he would not permit the demons to speak, because they knew him" (Mark 1:34).

"And he strictly ordered them [unclean spirits] not to make him known" (Mark 3:12).

"And he charged them [the cured] to tell no one; but the more he charged them, the more zealously they proclaimed it" (Mark 7:36).

"And as they were coming down the mountain, he charged them to tell no one what they had seen, until the Son of Man should have risen from the dead" (Mark 9:9).

Why didn't Jesus want His mission known? Why did He ask others to keep secret what they knew about Him? One very practical reason is that the people had a wrong idea of what the Messiah should be. Jesus felt that He must first change their thinking on the subject. Then He could bring them to see His role as Messiah.

THEY WANTED A CROWN, NOT A CROSS

The people of Christ's day thought of the Messiah as a warlike king who would storm the forts of the Romans and restore Israel to national glory. They wanted a David, not a Christ. They wanted a crown, not a cross. They wanted a glory that was secular in tone, not the divine glory that would appear in Jesus. They preferred the grandeur of a temple to the humble path of a pilgrim Church.

You should also keep in mind the distinction the Bible makes between a secret and a mystery. There is no secret once the cat is out of the bag. But the mystery remains, even after the secret is revealed. The biblical word for "reveal" should not be used in the ordinary sense of making known a piece of information. "Revealing," in the biblical sense, is not like the Associated Press quoting the latest bulletin from the White House. When the mystery of the person of Christ was revealed to His disciples, it still remained a mystery. Once a secret is made public, it ceases to be a secret. But you can't "make public" a mystery. No mystery is open to public inspection, even if it is preached from the housetops.

Judas may have made an "off the record" statement to the high priest about the messiahship of Jesus, but he did not, and could

THE APOSTLES *received the personal teaching of Jesus, yet they too could only grasp the full meaning of His mission by faith*

not, make known the mystery of it. The high priest remained in total ignorance of it. Pilate made public the news that Jesus was king of the Jews. He had a sign painted with that information and had it placed over the cross. But bulletin boards are not the way to make known the marvelous mystery of the inner kingship of Jesus. In fact, those who stood at the foot of the cross apparently never came to understand this mystery.

CHRIST'S SECRET CAN ONLY BE KNOWN BY FAITH

The mystery of the messiahship of Jesus cannot be made known by a press release. This is one of the deeper reasons why Jesus refused to allow the mystery of His mission to be common gossip in the streets. It was too profound a reality to be cheapened by this method.

The meaning of Jesus is not made known by the disclosure of a secret. We are dealing, here, with revelation. God reveals Himself to man only by veiling the brightness of His true glory. This is done out of kindness to men, for mortal men would be blinded by the direct light of God's glory. There is no direct vision of God. This sight would sear our eyes. In Jesus Christ, the divine truth veiled its brightness in the robe of human nature. God revealed Himself by hiding Himself in our humanity.

Jesus was so perfectly human that men in every age have looked on Him as one of their own. Often, they failed to look beyond the humanity He assumed. The theme of Jesus hidden in humanity has appeared in all the literature of Christendom since New Testament days. The beggar to whom Saint Martin of Tours gave his cloak was really Jesus. In Tolstoy's beautiful story, *Where Love Is God Is,* all the people that the shoemaker served were Christ. Even today, the Benedictine Rule says that one must receive the stranger at the door as if He were Christ.

So, the real reason why Jesus did not want to turn His life into a piece of public relations property is that *faith,* not the news media, is the true approach to the meaning of His life. At the heart of the meaning of Jesus lies a great mystery. You must have an open and sincere faith to be able to say "Amen" to that reality. You cannot cheapen it by a textbook, a test, a movie, or the hammering voice of a teacher. When you are at the very threshold of the meaning of Jesus, you arrive at the most sacred of moments. This calls for the kind of hush you would have when seeing mountains for the first time, or on entering a secret valley untouched by man.

THE WAY TO TELL OTHERS ABOUT THE MYSTERY OF JESUS

Naturally, the meaning of Jesus can be discussed and taught. But letting the secret out this way does not solve the problem. His mystery may still be beyond us, just as it was beyond Pilate and the high priest. Information alone is not the guarantee of faith. Caiaphas, the high priest, had the facts on who Jesus was, but he did not believe.

You may shout to nonbelievers that Jesus is the Messiah, but you will soon find out they may say to you: "So, what else is new?" The best method for letting out the secret is your commitment to love—Christ's kind of love (*see* page 267). The glory of God appears to others when Christian love is perfectly practiced. The real news to shout from the housetops is that Christians know how to form a community; they know how to cherish friendship and how to celebrate love. This is news that communicates the mystery of Jesus and challenges the world to have faith in Him.

THE GLORY OF THE LORD SHINES ON THE HOLY MOUNTAIN

The Transfiguration

Apparently, shrines are never out of date. We have the Hall of Fame for baseball and football, the graves of presidents, and the homes of generals. Religious shrines still remain at the top of tourist lists. Millions of people troop to Lourdes, Rome, and the old cathedrals of Europe every year. Muslims still journey to Mecca, and Jews visit the Wailing Wall in Jerusalem. The line of people waiting to view Lenin's tomb in Red Square shows no sign of letting up, even all these years after his death.

WHY DO WE BUILD SHRINES?

Building shrines is an old habit, deeply rooted in men. Building a shrine is a way of saying that something special has happened. The shrine preserves the memory. Its architecture is a language that preserves the beauty of a precious experience — whether it be the stirring plays of a quarterback, the victorious strategy of a general, or the graceful heritage of a saint.

WHAT HAPPENED TO JESUS AT THE TRANSFIGURATION?

In the story of the transfiguration of Jesus, something special happened. Peter, James, and John experienced the remarkable glory of Jesus. If ever divinity broke through a human person, it did so here, in Jesus. Peter, James, and John came to the unmistakable conclusion that God was in Christ in a way unmatched and unheard of in any other person in history. It was only natural that Peter wanted to build three shrines to capture the memory of the event for generations to come. Then all men would remember Jesus, whose face shone as the sun, and Moses the lawgiver, and Elijah the fiery prophet.

The transfiguration was God's way of ratifying the apostles' belief that Jesus is the Messiah. In Jewish tradition, it was felt that the Messiah would be a prophet similar to Moses. "The Lord your God will raise up for you a prophet like me [Moses] from among you, from your brothers—him you should heed . . . I will raise up for them a prophet like you [Moses] from among their brothers; and I will put my words in his mouth, and he shall speak to them all that I command him" (Deuteronomy 18:15, 18).

JESUS THE NEW MOSES

This is why there is such a strong parallel with Moses in the transfiguration event. The mount of the transfiguration is like a new Sinai. The Gospel writers do not identify the mountain, for they had little interest in geography. Tradition places the event at Mount Tabor which is in northern Israel, near the Sea of Galilee.

Jesus, the new Moses, heard the voice of God on the holy mountain. Peter wrote about this in his second letter: "For when he received honor and glory from God the Father and the voice was borne to him by the Majestic Glory, 'This is my beloved Son, with whom I am well pleased,' we heard this voice borne from heaven, for we were with him on the holy mountain" (2 Peter 1:17–18).

MOSES AND ELIJAH. *At the transfiguration Jesus was presented in terms of
the prophet who was similar to Moses
and Elijah—they represented the old
dispensation of which Christ is the
fulfillment*

We can compare this event to God speaking to Moses in the book
of Exodus: "The glory of the Lord settled on Mount Sinai, and the
cloud covered it *six days:* and on the seventh day He called to
Moses out of the midst of the cloud" (Exodus 24:16). Mark points
out the parallel: "And after *six days* Jesus took with him Peter
and James and John, and led them up a high mountain apart by
themselves; and he was transfigured before them" (Mark 9:2).

When Moses came down from Sinai, the skin of his face shone
so brightly that the people of Israel could scarcely look at him.
When Jesus came down from the holy mount after the transfiguration, the multitude who ran to meet Him were "greatly amazed"
(Mark 9:15).

The voice from the cloud had said, "This is my beloved Son;
listen to him." (Mark 9:7.) This is a duplication of what was said
of Moses in Deuteronomy: "Him you shall heed." Here, indeed,
in Jesus is the prophet similar to Moses.

ELIJAH WAS A SECOND MOSES

At the transfiguration, Jesus was presented in terms of the prophet who was similiar to Moses. In Jewish thought, Elijah also was a second Moses (*see* page 125). Like Moses, Elijah fought for the law of God. He, too, encountered God on Mount Horeb, which was another name for Mount Sinai (1 Kings 19:8). He was Moses over again. In Jewish legend neither Moses nor Elijah died, but were carried up to heaven. In ancient writings outside the Bible, you can find the story of the ascension of Moses. And you are probably familiar with the tale of the fiery chariot that transported Elijah to heaven (2 Kings 2:11–12).

Moses and Elijah represent the old order of things. They are presented, in the transfiguration account, as a contrast to the new Church represented by Christ. After the testimony from the voice in heaven, Moses and Elijah vanished. Then the apostles saw no one but Jesus. He brought full meaning to the realities that were only in shadow form at the time of the holy men, Moses and Elijah.

PETER'S PROPOSAL TO BUILD SHRINES

Many people like to think that Peter's statement about the shrines was a foolish remark mumbled because of his confusion at the marvelous sight of Jesus transfigured. This is far from the truth. Popular Jewish thought was that, when the Messiah came, he would be enshrined among his people. "My dwelling place shall be with them; and I will be their God, and they shall be my people" (Ezekiel 37:27). "And I will dwell in the midst of you, says the Lord" (Zechariah 2:10). Saint John made this application to Christ when he said "And the Word became flesh and dwelt among us, full of grace and truth" (John 1:14).

Peter was growing in his awareness that the time was near for the Messiah to take permanent residence among men. What Peter did not know is that the passion had to come before this could take place. Saint Luke, in his Gospel, brings out what Peter did not yet fully grasp. Moses and Elijah talked with Jesus about His departure—His death—at Jerusalem (Luke 9:31). The real shrine to Christ that would be His permanent residence—the Church— would come after the passion. Only a resurrected Christ could live in such a shrine.

DEATH AND TRANSFIGURATION

So the theme of death goes along with transfiguration. Death would come before the permanent transfiguration. This cycle of death and transfiguration continues today. There is a rhythm of darkness and light in the Church. People today speak of the death of the old Church and the emergence of the new. The Church we have inherited from the Council of Trent (1545–63) is undergoing many changes. The essentials remain, but the outer shell of the Church is getting a new look.

Today we have to be careful to preserve all that was genuine and faithful to the true Church of Christ, even as we work to find new forms for the Church in our time. Nowadays, we—the Church—are in the period of the passion and death. We stand under the darkness of the cross, awaiting a new transfiguration. Don't be discouraged. Remember, we know that our Redeemer lives and that He stands in glory. In our flesh, we shall see God. Let us build the shrine as Peter stated. That is, let us go forward to make a new transfiguration of Jesus possible in our time for the glory of God and the salvation of men.

CHRIST DIED FOR FOUR FREEDOMS
His Truth Shall Make You Free

Few people like to face unpleasant decisions. It is no pleasure for a judge to pronounce the death sentence. Heart patients tremble when they decide whether or not to have complicated heart surgery. What doctor likes to tell a person that he has cancer? What foreman enjoys telling a man that he is fired from his job?

CHRIST'S DECISION: TO DIE FOR MAN'S FREEDOM

Jesus, too, belongs to the brotherhood of men who have had to make very unpleasant decisions. Jesus committed Himself to a course of action that ultimately led to His death. He chose a path that would make His life's work appear to be a total failure. And who, in his right mind, would wish to crown his life's work with the stamp of failure?

Saint Luke recalls Christ's decision with these words: "When the days drew near for him to be received up, he *set his face* to go to Jerusalem" (Luke 9:51). These words introduce the theme of Christ's decision to be willing to die for His cause. They also begin what is often called "Luke's travel document." From chapters nine to nineteen, Luke describes the journey of Jesus from Galilee to Jerusalem. This description is meant to be more than mere geography.

Christ's journey to Jerusalem is like an exodus trip. It is a paschal procession. Jesus repeats, in His own life, the pilgrimage of the ancient people of God through death and deliverance (*see* page 66).

It takes a powerful purpose to move someone to be willing to die for a cause. Jesus was willing! He wanted to bring men freedom. He wished to set men free from slavery, whether it be slavery of the world, of the law, of sin, or of death. This is the dream to which He committed Himself and which He leaves to us as a heritage. It is a dream that has become a reality for all those who walk the same path as Jesus.

THE SLAVERY OF THE WORLD

His decision would bring men freedom from the domination of the world. The word "world" has two meanings in the gospel. There is the *neutral* world, which is simply the stage on which our lives are acted out. There is also the *hostile* world, where life is a state of siege against God. We may love the neutral world, but we must hate the hostile world.

We can love the neutral world, for that is the place where we work out our responsibilities. We must be responsible for the care of the earth. We must exercise care for the poor, the weak, and those treated unjustly. We can rejoice in scientific developments that improve man's lot in life. We are responsible *to* God *for* this earth.

We must hate the hostile world in the sense that we must refuse to commit ourselves to anything that tells us we have no responsibility to God. A world which wants to blot out God is not for us. Jesus waged war against a world such as this. It was this hostile world that put Him on the cross. Yet, in suffering at its hands, Jesus overcame this kind of world and rose from the dead. We, too, may suffer at the hands of the hostile world, but our pain can lead to our victory over it. Jesus has won for us freedom from this hostile world. We are free to work the earth for God's glory and the happiness of man.

THE SLAVERY OF THE LAW

When we say that Christ set us free from the law we must be clear about the sense in which this is meant: He set us free from the slavery of law. A law is wrong if nothing can be above it. A law is evil if it keeps men children. Laws lose their value when they take decisions out of men's hands. A Christian is freed from slavery to it. Only in this sense did Jesus set us free from the law. He did not abolish laws. He said that He came to fulfill—that is, give full meaning to—the law, not destroy it. Law is still necessary as a guideline for social and moral behavior. The younger you are, the more you need law for growth in discipline and a vision of what a good life means.

THE SLAVERY OF SIN

Jesus brought us freedom from sin. This can mean many things. We can see sin as a refusal to admit the presence of God in the life around us. Sin means much more than this, but let us consider this one aspect. Basically, sin is blindness to the action of God in current history. Sin is like saying that man is really alone in the world: God is not on the scene. Sin is like thinking that if He exists at all, He does not care about what is going on. At best, it sees God as a kindly clock-watcher; at worst, it sees Him as a cranky judge who lets the whole world go to hell in a mire of wars, disease, and suffering.

Jesus has freed us from thinking like this. In God, there is an ultimate concern for every human being on this earth. He is the basis for all our hopes and strivings. He is closely present in every effort of man to build a new creation. If anyone is supreme en-

JESUS *made a deliberate decision to die for man's freedom*

couragement, it is God. Jesus has introduced a new age in which
God is permanently living with men.

FREEDOM FROM DEATH

Finally, Jesus has assured us of freedom from death. Perhaps
it is better to say that He frees us from too great a concern for this
world. Christians die like other men. The difference should be in
the attitude. Death for the faithful Christian is a beginning, not an
end. We believe we shall survive death. A nonbeliever can have
two ways of handling death. He can become reckless and simply
throw his life away, or he can desperately hold on to life as tightly
as possible. Each way is an exaggeration.

The Christian is neither foolishly reckless about life, nor compulsive in holding on to it. The Christian lives life responsibly. Since he trusts in his survival, why shouldn't he take a responsible and joyous hold on the life that is here? In this way, he prepares for the life that is to come. It will be, simply, the fullness of what has already begun here on earth.

As we said, Jesus made the unpleasant decision to die for His cause. His primary reason was to bring us the four freedoms that we mentioned: freedom from the slavery of the world; freedom from the law in the sense we described; freedom from sin; and freedom from death. This is the truth of Christ that shall make you free. Discover this freedom and you will know what it means to live the most meaningful life.

LOVE AND MERCY THAT KNOW NO BOUNDS
The Prodigal Son

There is so much literature today about juvenile delinquents. Most of it is a lament. Little of it concerns the rescue and restoration of these young people to normal conditions of life. We are flooded with statistics on how much they steal, how often they drink, and the extent of their participation in drugs. Where are the statistics on the numbers who have repented or have been reformed?

GOD'S LOVE FOR SINFUL MANKIND

The story of the prodigal son concerns a delinquent boy. It also tells of his happy return to the family. Read the story in Luke's Gospel (15:11–32). Here we have a narrative that lends itself to many different applications. The common interpretation is more than sufficient.

The prodigal son is sinful mankind. The father is God. The people with whom he wasted his money represent the sinful world. Eating with the pigs is a sign of the degradation of sin. The elder brother in the story is the self-righteous Christian who really does not grasp the meaning of the mercy of God. And, we should remember, "prodigal" means wasteful.

In a way, the story should be called the prodigal father because of the boundless love and mercy he shows his son. In a sense, he has so much that it seems almost wasted. But this is only a way of speaking. One thing is sure, the father never ceases to love his son. Every day the boy is gone, the father goes out to look for him.

When the boy returns home, the father doesn't even wait for any kind of explanation. He doesn't even demand a confession of guilt from the son. The father surrounds the boy with signs of affection. Embracing the son who was dead and is now alive, he gives him a new robe, a chain, and a ring. He kills the best animal and orders a banquet. Let the musicians sing and the people dance. My boy is home!

THE ELDER BROTHER'S ATTITUDE

Only one element mars this scene of joy. The elder brother refuses to take part. After all, he has been the faithful son. He did not waste his inheritance. He stayed home and worked. His money did not go down the drain for gambling, wild women, and nights out on the town. He avoided scandal. There was no need for his father to be ashamed of his conduct. How could his father give approval to his younger brother by all this celebrating?

Of course, the younger boy should be forgiven. But let him first know his place. Punish him first. Let him serve time before he is given official forgiveness. The penalty will help him realize the depth of his faults and sins. Giving him a party like this will only serve to spoil him. He will never realize how serious was the shame he brought on the family.

What made the elder brother all the more peeved was that the father had never given such a party for him. It was almost as though infidelity was rewarded and fidelity was ignored. The elder brother had never failed his father, and in the logic of rewards and punishments, he deserved such a celebration.

WHICH BROTHER IS MORE CHRISTIAN?

I have sometimes asked young people which brother they would prefer to have as a friend. The majority have always said they would choose the elder brother. This was their first reaction. Partly, I think, they felt this was the expected answer to give a priest. After all, shouldn't I be on the side of the "good guys"? The elder brother was the just man. He was the correct one. Shouldn't he be chosen? Then I press the question further. Which brother seems more human? Which one ultimately is more Christian? On second reflection, the young people usually say they would prefer the younger boy as a friend. He had human weaknesses. But he also had the *humility* to want to confess his sin to his father and return home as a servant in the house.

Then I ask them which one rejected salvation. At first, it seems that neither one did. The elder brother was a morally correct man, and so seems to be already saved. The younger one has repented of his sins and so is also saved. But then the story says that the elder brother refused to go into his father's house. The father's house is the Church. The Church is the community of those who enter the way of salvation. To consciously refuse to belong to this community is to refuse salvation.

THE "RESPECTABLE" PEOPLE AND THE "SINNERS"

The really sad part of this story is that the apparently just man has deliberately excluded himself from the community of faith. The elder brother, who on the surface of things is a "good Catholic," has, in fact, quietly left his father's house. His idea of religion is too narrow. He is unable to accept the incredibly wide mercy of God. His God is too small!

People like the elder brother are not absent from the Church

THE PRODIGAL SON *said "Father, I have sinned against heaven
and against you. I no longer deserve to be called your son."
But his father clasped him in his arms and kissed him tenderly*

today. We have many apparently just parishioners sitting in the pews of our churches, self-righteously looking down on sinners. They abhor both the sinner and the socially unacceptable. But this is in opposition to the mercy shown by the father in the parable. This attitude is out of step with Christ's own example of associating with outcasts and sinners. Today, we don't talk so much about sinners as we do about the socially unacceptable. They may include peace protesters, Negroes, Jews, and bearded folk wearing sneakers. These are the security risks. Eating with them would spoil our status. Are we sure that Jesus, who associated with sinners and outcasts in His time, would not eat with these "sinners" today?

We are not talking about a matter of restaurants. We are saying that Jesus has a sense of human compassion far wider than the ordinary. To Him, every human being is a pearl of great price — even if that person lives in the twilight zone of society. Jesus associates with such people so that He can discover the beauty in them and enlighten their sense of human dignity. He communicates with them so that He might restore their hope, and ease their entrance into the kingdom of God. To have this courage we need the alertness and fidelity of God Himself. It is no small matter to oppose the unChristian ideas of those with whom we work and associate. It is all too easy for the "saved Christian" to forget the poor, scorn anyone who is different, and ignore the consequences of prejudice.

JESUS MIXED WITH SINNERS TO SHOW THE LORD'S MERCY

Jesus made the mercy of the Lord an intensely personal affair. Religion for Him was not simply a slick pattern. It was more than learning a few abstract ideas in religion class or writing out a check for charity. He knew there were annoying and embarrassing aspects to religion. He did not flinch from these. He entered the brotherhood of men. He knew full well how many of His brothers had taken the heritage of the earth and wasted it in sinful ways.

He came to tell them about the mercy of the Father. He brought the sacraments of reconciliation and love. He invited the sinners to eat the greatest banquet of all, the Eucharist. He did not pout outside the dinner hall. He Himself was the host at the meal. And these are some of the splendid lessons of the story of the prodigal son.

CHRIST'S KINGDOM HAS COME: A NEW AGE
The Last Judgment Story

It is not likely that a young person will really take a lot of time out to think about the last judgment or the end of the world. This does not seem to fit in with the "now" generation. Are those who just stepped on the threshold of life going to have a vision of the last things? Does the girl who has not yet seen the beauty of the world look ahead to the decline of the world? Does the boy who still stretches to be taller than Dad think of the day when his own son will edge him out of the center of things?

THE LAST JUDGMENT STORY IN THE GOSPELS

The Gospels appear to be talking about the physical end of the world. Generally, this is what people think when hearing the "judgment Gospel" of the Last Sunday after Pentecost. No question but that this is the most chilling Gospel we hear during the Church year. It meant a lot to the people of the late Middle Ages who suffered under the Black Plague, which brought a vision of death so severe that it seemed like the last judgment itself. Perhaps the Christians of Hiroshima hear this Gospel with vital interest.

But there is another way of looking at the last judgment story. It could well be referring more to the collapse of the old religion, than to dissolving mountains, falling stars, and bloody moons. Read the judgment story in Matthew, chapter 24.

Picture Jesus and the apostles climbing the Mount of Olives, which is a hill overlooking the city of Jerusalem and its crown, the temple. While they gaze on the glory of the city of David and the splendor of the second temple, the apostles ask Jesus about the end of all this. "Tell us, when will this be, and what will be the sign of your coming and the close of the age?" (Matthew 24:3). Note the expression, "close of the age." This doesn't mean the end of time, but the end of a period of history.

THE JEWS' UNDERSTANDING OF TIME

It is no easy thing for a person of today, who is clock conscious, to appreciate the way time was understood by the Jews. Of course, they were aware of clock time, marking off the sections of the day as the third, sixth, and ninth hours. But time as the mere measurement of the length of a day or week or year was less important to them than time which expressed the *quality* of life.

You may recall how in the Christmas story there is much talk about the "fullness of time." John the Baptist preached about the "acceptable time." Time really assumed importance when it signified a change in the quality of the people's way of life. Clock time did not mean so much for them since things were very much the same from day to day. One day was as predictable as another.

This difference is still true today. We speak of a "good time Charley," of having a "bad time of it." There is the athlete who realizes the time has come for him to put his best foot forward. We also think in terms of time that have less to do with the clock and more to do with the meaning of life.

JESUS *taught the apostles that His kingdom has now come, that the new age has arrived with all its possibilities of grace and love and forgiveness*

HOW DID CHRIST DESCRIBE THE "CLOSE OF THE AGE"?

So, the apostles asked Jesus about the "close of the age." When would the judgment come, and the judge appear? Jesus told them the beginning of the end of the age would come in their own lifetime. He warned them about being led astray by fake messiahs. He mentioned the violence they could expect. To reinforce His point, He used a two-toned language — realistic and poetic.

His realistic description had scenes of persecution, screaming mothers, fiery hatred, famines, and earthquakes. This uproar would be accompanied by the beginning of an incredible expansion of the gospel.

To make this more dramatic, Jesus turned to poetry. The catastrophe that marked the end of the age would be as dreadful as falling stars, red moons, and black suns. Jesus borrowed this vocabulary of violence from a school of poets known as apocalyptic writers. The word "apocalypse" means "revelation." The poets of this school usually became popular when tragedies hit a nation. Their technique was to use natural disasters to describe the disasters of history. The reason I point this out to you is that Christ's words about the trouble in the heavens are not to be taken literally. He used this language to show how serious the problem accompanying the end of an age would be.

JESUS BRINGS THE NEW AGE OF LOVE AND FORGIVENESS

The "close of an age" doesn't happen easily. Christ's new Church would be a radical departure from the old. That is why Jesus says the kingdom of heaven — that is, the Church — suffers violence, and only the violent bear it away.

Jesus speaks of the arrival of the new age as a coming of the "Son of Man in the clouds." This doesn't mean you should strain your eyes scanning the skies for some mysterious figure. This image of the Son of Man riding the skies is borrowed from the book of Daniel, chapter 7. There, Daniel has a dream in which he sees the old age condemned by God and a new one introduced by a *real man*, that is, one whose face is turned toward God in obedience. Placing this real man in the heavens was a way of saying that he was responsive to God's creative power and wisdom. (*see* page 166).

Jesus is teaching us that He is the real man who is totally obedient to the Father and is the living example of His creative power and wisdom. Jesus ushers in the new age with all its possibilities of grace and love and forgiveness. Historically, the final close of the age was symbolized by the destruction of Jerusalem and the temple in the year A.D 70. Poetically, the close of the age came with the confusion and sorrow suffered by those who were too rigid to accept the new kingdom, which occurred in the death and glorification of Jesus.

CHRIST'S KINGDOM HAS COME

So, the last judgment story is not a doomsday tale. It is not a way of saying, "Watch out or the bomb will get you." The story is not used to scare Christians into repentance, but to celebrate the reality of the new age in which Christians live. *The judge has come. His kingdom is here.* The last judgment is a call to Christians to accept the present kingdom and the test of love which is its citizenship.

Our lives are a statement of how we react to that kingdom. The awesome element is not a frightening judge, but the splendor of victorious love which is awaiting our acceptance. Rather than fear, we should sing out: *"Come Lord Jesus!"*.

SAINT MATTHEW'S STORY OF CHRIST'S PASSION

The Moment of Decision: His Agony in the Garden

All of the Gospels tell the story of the passion of Jesus. Each writer brings to this central event in Jesus' life a particular mood and meaning. First, we shall discuss Saint Matthew's approach. Then we shall turn our attention to the account in Saint John.

EMPHASIS ON THE HISTORY OF THE PASSION

Matthew emphasizes the historical aspect of Christ's passion. The length of his passion narrative, however, is so great that we can only ponder some of the points he raises. His account of the agony in the garden deserves our first attention. Matthew makes it clear this is *the* moment of decision for Jesus. Christ would have to risk losing all to gain the freedom He wanted for men.

Jesus had carefully trained His followers and built up a wide reputation for being a merciful healer. He was honored as a superb preacher. People were saying that He was a great prophet, just like Moses. He had gained greater prestige than the high priest and the Roman governor. We could compare this prestige, today, to someone considered more important than a pope and a president combined. Jesus was at the peak of His career. On Palm Sunday, the crowds had welcomed Him to Jerusalem with honors ordinarily reserved for monarchs. This was the tragedy of His situation. He would now have to put Himself in a position that would cost Him the support of the people, and would permit His enemies to direct all their hostility against Him. He would have to stand alone.

HOSTILITY OF THE RELIGIOUS LEADERS

The religious leaders were jealous of Jesus' popularity and enraged at His teachings. He was attacking individual members of the institutional Church of His day, and was threatening its very existence. In saying the kingdom was at hand, he was sentencing the old Church to extinction. In cleansing the temple and talking about the destruction of Jerusalem, He was, in effect, clearly announcing that He was making room for the new Church.

How could this man be so bold, the religious leaders wondered. How could He dare to suggest that this venerable religion, brought into being by God Himself, was now about to pass away? What were His credentials? How could He prove He was a prophet? Who did He think He was? By what right did He act, they asked one another.

As far as the religious leaders of His day were concerned, Jesus was, plainly, a heretic. It was bad enough that He proposed teachings that differed from their views. What made Him more dangerous was His plan to replace Judaism itself with a new Church.

THE RELIGIOUS LEADERS' POINT OF VIEW

In one sense, it is not hard to sympathize with the religious leaders' point of view. They were being asked to swallow a very bitter pill. They had been accustomed to acting as the sole guardians of the truth. They were not used to hearing sermons from the

PILATE *said:* "*I am innocent of this man's blood. It is your concern.*" At this, the crowd cried out: "*His blood be on us and on our children*" (Matthew 27:24–25)

common people. And they certainly did not think that an upstart lay preacher from a little unimportant town in Galilee should accuse them of being hypocritical, let alone being unfaithful to the law of Moses. Even the most honest and humble among them found it hard to be open to the message of Jesus.

Christ was aware of all this when He was in the garden of His agony. He knew that while He had excited the joyful admiration of the people, He had also pushed the religious leaders to the breaking point. He realized that His only choice now was to let them crush Him. He must permit them to ruin His reputation and lead Him to a scandalous death. He was walking into the most dangerous of all forms of human outrage, the anger that rises from religious fanaticism. The blazing hostility of the establishment would break out and destroy Him.

If Jesus were to turn to any texts of the Old Testament for comfort at that moment, it would be to the poems about the suffering servant of Yahweh (Isaiah 42:1–4 and 53). That eloquent figure in the book of Isaiah chose to take upon himself the guilt of the world. He would be like a quiet lamb led to the slaughter (*see* page 140).

WHY NOT TAKE POWER BY FORCE?

Jesus trusted that, in His death, the guilt of men would find forgiveness, and that He Himself would discover a new existence. These are the two points that sustained Jesus in that dark hour. His submission to the wrath of the old Church and the sword of Rome would really achieve a blessed freedom for mankind and He Himself would rise from the dead.

That is why Jesus really sweated blood. It was not just from the fear of pain and humiliation, but also because of the dreadful risk that He was taking. Why should He give up all at the peak of His career? Why not organize the obvious popular support He had recently gained? Why not become a sort of rabble-rouser, urging the crowds to storm the temple and install Him as the high priest? Then He would hold the reins of power and could negotiate with the Roman governor.

Jesus could not do this because the kingdom of God must arrive by the road of the humble and the weak. It was not to be installed through the methods of worldly power. The weak were to confound the strong, not the other way around. "God chose what is foolish in the world to shame the wise, God chose what is weak in the world to shame the strong" (1 Corinthians 1:27).

Saint Matthew makes it clear that Jesus was the real fulfillment of the suffering servant of Yahweh that Isaiah foretold. Jesus wished to work for salvation as a servant of mankind, not as a dictator. He did not accept the cheap victory He could have gotten immediately with the support of the crowd. He wanted the long-range permanent victory that would come only by taking the road of apparent defeat. How often He had said in His lifetime that he who would save his life could expect to lose it. Now, during His agony in the garden, Jesus made His own personal decision in accordance with this teaching. He chose to lose His life.

EVERY CHRISTIAN COMES TO HIS OWN AGONY IN THE GARDEN

Every Christian, eventually, comes to his own agony in the garden. Every Christian faces the prospect of the passion. If he refuses to enter these events, he rejects Christianity. Our baptism announced that we were willing to participate in the passion of Jesus. In the context of our lives, this claim must be worked out. The details vary with each individual Christian. The moment of truth lies in store for every true Christian. How it will appear depends on the circumstances of time and place. This is the testing period. It involves risking all that we own. It is a risk that tests our selfishness, our worldliness, and our courage.

JESUS IN GETHSEMANE *made His own personal decision to take upon Himself the guilt of the world. Every Christian eventually comes to his own agony in the garden, when he must face the prospect of suffering for his decision to follow Christ*

The passion of the Christian ultimately is a test of *agape*— that love where there is no worry about return (*see* page 267). Jesus agonized through this decision and said "yes." What is your answer?

SAINT JOHN'S STORY OF CHRIST'S PASSION

Jesus Is the New Adam

In Saint Matthew's account of the passion, we saw Jesus as the suffering servant who chose humiliation to achieve salvation. In Saint John's account of the passion, we shall see Jesus as the second Adam who, as true king of the world, brings us the sacraments of salvation.

JESUS IS THE MAN ADAM FAILED TO BE

The garden scene in John's account does not concentrate on the agony. Through the use of symbolism, John brings out the idea of the garden as representing Eden, and Jesus as the new Adam (*see* page 22). The serpent in the garden of Jesus' agony is Judas, for "Satan entered into him" (John 13:27). The old Adam had lost control of himself in the garden, but Jesus now remains the master. By this He shows us what it means to be a real man. When the soldiers come to capture Him, they find themselves unable to touch Him until He permits it. He is the master of this situation.

The word "Adam" means man. Jesus emerges from the garden scene as the man Adam failed to be. Adam was supposed to be the guardian of the earth. He and Eve, in the words of a famous author, were to be the "Lords of the World." They failed. Jesus did not. Later, before Pilate, it is Jesus who stands regally in the court of Pilate. Jesus is the king. It is the Roman governor who is really on trial.

WHAT IS TRUTH?

In describing the scene with Pilate, John emphasizes Jesus' kingship (John 18:28–19:22). Being a king here means being a real man. Kingship is not a matter of crowns and jewels. Thrones, guards, and palaces can be dodges which obscure the true meaning of kingship. A true king is a man who has discovered the way to be thoroughly human.

Pilate, here, becomes the spokesman for the world. When he asks Jesus if He is a king, Pilate echoes the confused, but truly searching question of mankind: "What is truth?" (John 18:38). Ordinarily, we would have expected that worldly power should hold some claim to the meaning of truth. Now, the worldly power of the throne, represented by Pilate, looks anxiously, in its inadequacy, to Jesus who appears as man in the truest sense of the word — as God intended man to be.

CHRIST SAW TRUTH AS A WAY OF LIVING

To Pilate's question, "What is truth?" Jesus did not reply. Let us try to understand why He remained silent. Truth is not just a proposition. At the Last Supper, Thomas had asked Jesus to show the disciples the way to salvation. Jesus replied that He was the way, and that He was the truth. This was an important point. The *way* comes before the *truth*. In fact, the truth and the way are the same thing.

Jesus is not saying He *has* the truth, so much as He is claiming to *be* the truth. Truth is less a matter of ideas for the mind as it is a manner of living. Jesus paused when Pilate asked his famous question because He wanted the governor to look at a man, not listen to a philosophy. Jesus wished to help Pilate see that *truth is a way of living.* A person can have plenty of true ideas in his mind, but if they are never practiced, of what use are they?

Too often, Christians have forgotten the real reason for Christ's silence in the court of Pilate. Many Christians are content if they can tuck lots of truths away in their minds *about* Christ. They fail to realize that Christ saw truth as a way of living. If we live the truth, then knowing the truth makes some sense.

MARY AND CHRIST'S CHURCH

We see Jesus again as the new Adam at Calvary. Mary stands at the foot of the cross as a symbol of Eve. At Cana, Jesus called Mary "woman." As "woman," she had summed up in herself the faith of Israel and humbly said "Amen" to the work of her son, Jesus. At Calvary, He again calls her "woman." She is the Eve, the woman, who becomes truly the mother of all the living. She is the mother of those who are in grace.

The soldiers brought Jesus to the cross at the very hour that the lambs were being sacrificed in the temple. Now, the sacrifice of those animals has lost its meaning, for the old Church is dying. The temple veil will soon be torn apart. It is Jesus, the new lamb of God, who will be able to reconcile mankind to the Father. He speaks to the woman telling her that John is now her son. In John's account, Jesus symbolically points to Mary as the Church, with whom the faithful, like John, should join.

Then Jesus bowed His head and handed over His Spirit to His Church that will carry on His work. At this point, John adds the detail of the "spear thrust." In the image of the spear thrust, Jesus surrenders life itself in the cause of His call to love. He teaches us that a love like His love is as strong as death.

CHRIST'S CHALLENGE TO EVERY CHRISTIAN

John recalls for us the blood and water that flow from the side of Christ. Blood is the biblical image for life and the sacramental picture of the Eucharist. Running water is the sign of the new

ON CALVARY *Jesus Christ gave His life for love of mankind. He is the second Adam, the true king of the world, who brings us the sacraments of salvation*

creation and the sacrament of baptism. The scene of the spear thrust into Jesus' side is an insight into the fresh creation Jesus brings to this world with His death.

Jesus put His life on the line so that men might take seriously His call to Christian love. He allowed Himself to be brutally opened that men might begin to build the beautiful world where His kind of love is practiced. His open wounds cry out to men to build the beautiful city which ought to be the meaning of the Church in the world. In the symbolism of the cross, Jesus shows that Christian love truly exists.

Saint Matthew's story of the passion showed Jesus as the suffering servant who rejected the power of the world to achieve salvation. Saint John's story of the passion brings us the new Adam who walks to the cross as the living truth to show us how a real man should act. The suffering of the world calls for new suffering servants and real men to continue Christ's work in the world. This is the challenge Christ issues to every Christian in every age. Are you ready to take up His challenge, and show His kind of love to the world?

EASTER
Christian Freedom

Easter tells us that tears should be dried. Weeping should cease. Jesus has risen! He lives today and urges us to laugh and sing an alleluia. Let sorrow vanish for He has achieved His victory over death. Such is the meaning of the change in Mary Magdalene after her encounter with the risen Christ. She stood depressed at the empty tomb. Angels asked her why she wept and she told them it was because someone had taken away the body of her Lord. A "gardener" appeared and asked her why she wept. She asked him to show her the body of her Lord.

WE FIND THE LORD IN TEARS AND STRUGGLE

Here, Mary Magdalene represents fallen mankind which is faced with the prospect that its hope in Jesus might be crushed. Like Mary, men "return" to the empty tomb to look into the mystery of death. They quiz the Church, God's agent. They question the world's wisdom, which is represented by the gardener, the custodian of the earth.

Mankind, like Mary Magdalene, is not put off by the very mystery of Christ's empty tomb. Men continue to search for the body of their Lord. In the garden, Mary wept and searched and questioned.

JESUS APPEARS TO MARY MAGDALENE *after the resurrection, thus rewarding her for her hope*

"They have taken away my Lord, and I do not know where they have laid him. . . . Sir, if you have carried him away, tell me where you have laid him, and I will take him away" (John 20:13, 15).

THE REWARD OF HOPE

Mary was rewarded for not losing hope. Her search was successful. She reminds every Christian that finding the Lord is not easy. A strong personal effort is required to find the living body of Christ. This involves work, tears, and struggle. All of this we would prefer to avoid. Because Mary loved so much, all was forgiven. Because she loved so much, she is portrayed in the Gospels as the first to see Jesus after He had risen from the dead.

Jesus appeared to Mary Magdalene as a gardener, as a custodian of the earth and its fruits. The psalms say the whole earth is full of God's glory. Jesus appeared to her, not as a heavenly angel, but as an earthly man who had begun the new creation.

DEEP PERSONAL FRIENDSHIP WITH CHRIST

Jesus was a puzzle to Mary until He did what true love must eventually do, He said her name. He spoke to her, saying simply, "Mary." It is the privilege of genuine personal friendship to say the name of the beloved with a power that causes recognition and response. There is no disappointed hope here. We see that those who really look for the Lord will find Him. When they find Him, they are named. That is, they are made aware that they are more deeply known and loved than could be imagined. As God named the elements of the earth when He created them, so Jesus says our name each time we rediscover Him in our search for His presence among us.

Mary's discovery of the risen Christ brought her, also, to pronounce His name. She said, "Master." Having found Him again, she did not want to let Him go. But Jesus told her: "Do not hold me, for I have not yet ascended to the Father; but go to my brethren and say to them, I am ascending to my Father and your Father, to my God and your God" (John 20:17). He is, indeed, the gardener, the custodian of the earth. But His garden now is to be the whole universe. His mission is to be the Lord and hope of all creation.

THE RISEN CHRIST IS AVAILABLE TO ALL MEN

No one appearance of Christ is sufficient. No single group of persons, even Christians, can claim the risen Christ as their pri-

"HE HAS RISEN, *He is not here. Remember what He told you*
when He was still in Galilee, that the Son of Man had to be
handed over into the power of sinful men and be crucified,
and rise again on the third day?" (Luke 24:6-7)

vate preserve. The power and the glory of the risen Christ must be made known to all. The risen Christ is not a household God, quietly served by a few, even if those few are ardently devoted. If Christ's resurrection meant anything, it meant the permanence of His remarkable freedom. He is now completely available to all men.

Once Jesus could stroll only through the hills and valleys of Galilee, but now He is free to stride the course of history itself. It is this exciting freedom and availability that He wishes to share with everyone at Easter.

The first people to know this were the apostles. During the public ministry of Jesus, they had been a fickle lot at best. After the crucifixion, they huddled in fear behind closed doors. Their house was hardly the home of the brave and the free. But at Easter, something happened to them. Their fear drained away and was replaced with an enthusiastic boldness. Chattering teeth became smiles, and sweaty palms became hands firm in granting benediction in the name of Jesus.

THE MEANING OF EASTER FOR CHRISTIANS

All of a sudden, the apostles found that they experienced the same incredible freedom toward life that they had once noticed in Jesus. They could not have imitated this freedom, but they suddenly received it from the glorified Jesus. They had His Spirit. They were ready to spread His freedom and love to all mankind.

Mary Magdalene came to know this same freedom which the apostles experienced. Jesus told her, as He tells us, not to hold onto Him, but to follow Him instead. This was Mary Magdalene's Easter. It began with tears and ended with her joyful alleluia to the disciples: "I have seen the Lord!" (John 20:18).

As we struggle with our own personal frustrations in seeking Christ, we have much to identify with in the Magdalene story. Her search was rewarding and so ours will be. At Easter the world looks with curiosity at Christian gatherings. It can hear the happy songs and see the bright faces. Maybe, too, it will see the gardener and hear the name that speaks of godly love and human hope.

This will happen only if Christ's freedom is truly in us. The world needs more than a glimpse of enthusiastic worship. It must sense the contagious freedom of Jesus in Christians. The world cannot merely read about Easter in the religion section of our newspapers and magazines. It must read about Easter in the lives of Christians. If we are living an alleluia, then we are probably a witness to Easter. Jesus is risen. Alleluia!

THE MEANING OF THE ASCENSION
A Time for Christian Joy

The space age is turning the eyes of man to the heavens. The moon is merely the first of many thrilling conquests in space that lie ahead. Space journeys such as these provide helpful background for our understanding of the ascension of Jesus. Christ's entrance into space was a biblical way of describing His entrance into glory. As the *Apostles' Creed* expresses it: He sits at the right hand of the Father.

WHAT DOES THE ASCENSION MEAN?

All too often, the ascension of Jesus is misunderstood. People think of it as Jesus saying farewell to the world. But this is not true. In the ascension, Jesus becomes more profoundly present to the whole earth and the universe than was possible during His historical presence in Palestine.

During His earthly career, His presence was confined to the shores of Galilee and the hills of Judea. The ascension marks the release of His powerful presence, not just to all the fields and mountains of the earth, but also to the faraway moon and beyond into the space we've never even imagined.

Saint Paul spoke of this to his parishioners at Ephesus: "I do not cease to give thanks for you, remembering . . . that the God of our Lord Jesus Christ, the Father of glory . . . raised him [Christ] from the dead and made him sit at his right hand in the heavenly places, far above all rule and authority and power and dominion . . . he has put all things under his feet" (Ephesians 1:16, 17, 20–22).

JESUS IS LORD OF THE WHOLE UNIVERSE

The ascension is a way of saying that Jesus is not just Lord of the Church, but of the whole universe as well. The Father has entrusted to Jesus the power of wisely governing the history and spiritual hope of mankind. Christ touches the very course of the universe itself. The heavens and the earth are full of His glory.

In the mystery of the ascension, we celebrate the fact that our Father has provided in Jesus an intelligent and optimistic purpose for the unfolding of nature and history. Neither the earth nor the universe is rolling back toward a black destiny. For over all is the touch of Jesus who loves the earth and its people. It is His love that calls everyone and everything to find its fulfillment. It is because He loves us first that we can respond and feel the welcome to move forward.

Because Christ has ascended, people can operate more confidently in their tasks. He gives to men an assurance that He is a constructive Savior who is close to the moments of human decisions. The ascension is, therefore, a summons to a positive view of the future. Jesus has entered into the very life of the human situation. Another way of putting it: He is inside, a vital part of human direction.

WE SHARE IN CHRIST'S LORDSHIP OVER THE UNIVERSE

As mankind adventurously begins to explore space, it should be known that this is done with the invitation of Christ to explore

JESUS *went with His disciples to the vicinity of Bethany and blessed them. "While He blessed them He withdrew from them and was carried up to heaven"* (Luke 24:51)

the potential of the human spirit and intelligence. Scientific research, universal education, social progress are all echoes of an approving Christ, who nods as did His Father in Genesis: Well done! (*see* Genesis 1).

This is what is meant when it is said that we are called to share in Christ's lordship over all reality. We have received His Holy Spirit who takes us out of this world and brings us into the age to come. What does this mean? It means that the Holy Spirit liberates us from having a narrow and intolerant view of the meaning of life. Instead of wearing blinders or rose colored glasses, we share with the people of God the forward-looking insight of the Lord Himself.

THE ASCENSION: A TIME FOR CHRISTIAN JOY

The ascension is a time for Christian joy. The Church sings: "Lift up your heads, O gates! and be lifted up, O ancient doors! that the King of glory may come in. Who is this King of glory? The Lord, strong and mighty, the Lord, mighty in battle! Lift up your heads, O gates . . . that the King of glory may come in" (Psalm 24:7–9).

This psalm pictures the ascension of Christ in terms of a triumphal procession into a walled city. The gates are thrown open in joy at the arrival of the victorious leader. Christians should open the gates of their hearts so that the feeling of the universal victory of Christ's love might enter in.

True, ours is the dilemma of knowing Christ's victory while not yet having it fully made a part of our lives. He won, but we don't express His victory. It is our job to make His victory visible for all men. When the world looks at Christians, it should find people who are not narrow-minded. It should discover a community that doesn't rest on its past laurels. It should find a group of restless men full of holy impatience. This community looks to the future and its immense possibilities for the happiness of mankind.

Ascension Christians are not grouchy, perpetually pouting. Pessimism is not their cup of tea. If ever optimism is shown in this dark world, it should be in the community of ascension Christians. Hope, not despair, is their theme song.

EACH NEW GENERATION HAS NEW CHALLENGES

Ascension Christians know what courage means. They live their lives to the full because they understand the value of taking risks. They reject the religion of the rut, the routine. They realize that each new generation has its own challenges calling for new solutions. They are aware that the shape of Christian faith takes fresh forms in every age. Perhaps at one time it was converting the barbarians, preserving classical culture, and forging a unifying creed. In past times Christian faith fought heresy, sent missionaries to China, and elaborated a calendar of saints. Within our own memory, it constructed an astonishing school system, impressive parish plants, and a breathtaking membership reaching into every corner of the world.

Ascension Christians have done these things and must do more. Today, they must give new meaning to the word "tolerance." They must face the problems of world hunger, overpopulation, and strangled cities. These are the challenges to faith today. A true ascension Christian has this world view. He has the courage and will take the risks. "Lift up your gates. The King of glory is coming!"

PENTECOST
The Church on Fire

North America, of all places, has been the breeding ground for many strange religions. The last century saw the rise of the Shakers and the Holy Rollers. Today, only a handful of people practice these faiths, and their farms and meeting houses are quaint museums of past belief.

THESE SECTS HAVE A LESSON FOR US

But even today in the hills of Tennessee and Kentucky, people dance around, seemingly possessed of some spirit, and they reach into a box filled with poisonous snakes and pick one out and curl it around their necks, while shouting out words in a strange tongue. Surprisingly, few of the people are ever bitten. And nearly every state and province has its wandering healer, who sets up a tent or rents the local auditorium and leads his followers — usually the poor and the ignorant — in wildly emotional services.

Most of us are curious about these sects; some of us may even be amused. But they do have a lesson for us. These religions, in a general way, can show us the role of the Holy Spirit in the Church. Violent dancing, shaking, snake charming, speaking in tongues, healing — all of these happenings are an emotional, over-exaggerated form of the appearance of the Spirit in our own Church.

TWO OLD TESTAMENT STORIES

The Bible has many accounts of the seizure of the Spirit. Take the story of Samson, for instance (*see* page 84). The Israelites bound him with ropes and handed him over to the Philistines as a hostage to prevent war. But the Philistines taunted and tormented him beyond reason. At that point, "the Spirit of the Lord came mightily upon him, and the ropes which were on his arms became as flax that has caught fire" (Judges 15:14). The Spirit of God seized Samson, who picked up the jawbone of an ass and slew a thousand of the Philistines of this world. "With the jawbone of an ass . . . have I slain a thousand men" (Judges 15:16).

Another story of Spirit seizure is found in the account of Daniel in the lion's den (*see* page 164). The prophet had been there six days without food. God noticed the hunger of Daniel and prepared to help him through the services of the prophet Habakkuk.

> Now the prophet Habakkuk was in Judea: he had been making a stew, and breaking up bread small to put in a basket. He was on his way to the fields, taking this to the harvesters, when the angel of the Lord spoke to him, "Take the meal you are carrying to Babylon and give it to Daniel in the lion pit." "Lord," replied Habakkuk "I have not even seen Babylon, and know nothing about this pit." The angel of the Lord seized his head and carried him off by the hair to Babylon where, with a great thrust of his spirit, he set Habakkuk down on the edge of the pit [Daniel 14:33–36].

THE SPIRIT IN THE NEW TESTAMENT

The Old Testament stories of the seizures by the Spirit indicate that such occasions were rare, and generally happened only to special people. In the New Testament, the seizure by the Spirit is a constant experience of the Church. In the upper room at Pentecost there was a seizure by the Spirit. The power of God took hold of all the Church. It swept their inmost souls with a violent wind and loosened the darkness of their minds with the holy fire.

Outside in a vast square stood the people who represented the nations of the world. When the Spirit-seized Church strode into that square, all those divided people experienced a sensation of unity. St. Peter, inspired by the Spirit, preached Christ to them, and thousands "accepted what he said and were baptized" (Acts 2:41).

The artists of the Middle Ages loved to contrast the picture of the tower of Babel with the image of the upper room. Babel symbolized the fundamental divisions of men caused by selfishness and sin (*see* Genesis 11:1–9). Pentecost was the assurance that such division was no longer a tragic necessity for mankind. The seizure by the Spirit was a guarantee that the horizons of human unity are not merely a dream but a reality that can be achieved.

The sign of that unity in the city streets and village squares is the Church caught up in force by the Spirit of God. Pentecost was a day of the Lord in which the work of Jesus began to have the effect He had promised.

WHAT IS A CHARISM?

When a person is especially seized by the Spirit, we say that he has received a charism. Charism means anointing and implies a gift. Such a man is a charismatic. This word is used more frequently today than in many years. For example, President Kennedy's major biographers all claim that he was charismatic. The term has also been applied to Ghandi, Pope John, and Albert Schweitzer. This is a way of saying that these men walked on this earth with a special glow, an uncanny attractiveness, a charm that engaged men's hearts. In a sense, a "spirit" seized these men in an unaccountable way.

The list of charisms you could receive from the Spirit is remarkably full: faith, gift of healing, gift of prophecy, speaking in tongues, interpretation of tongues, prayers uttered in the Spirit, services of help, powers of administration, the Spirit's aid in important decisions, and celibacy. You can find this list of gifts in chapter 12 of Paul's first letter to the Corinthians.

PETER, *filled with the Holy Spirit, preached Christ to the multitude, and thousands were baptized*

THE SPIRIT AT WORK IN OUR TIMES

It seems fair to say that these gifts are appearing in abundance today. Pope Pius XII predicted that the Church would know a second spring in the second half of the twentieth century. His forecast seems to be right.

The Second Vatican Council was the heralding of that renewal which is the special work of the Spirit. The Bible calls such deeds a new creation. Journalists simply talk in terms of the new Church. Since the Council, other evidence suggests that the Spirit is strongly present with us today. Perhaps some signs of this are: the rapid growth of lay theologians, the emergence of the inner-city ministry, the phenomenon of religion as front-page news, the emphasis on commitment, honesty, and hope in Christian life. These and many other developments may signal a new burst of the Spirit's influence.

The Church is on fire today in a way that Jesus would want it to be. He said that He did not come to bring peace, but the sword. He came to set men on fire. Religion is not some sort of aspirin to calm people's nerves. A real Christianity, far from being tranquil, is a religion that disturbs the hypocritical, the lazy, the comfortable, and the faithless from their sleep. It rallies men to give their lives for justice and love. Such is the seizure of the Spirit of Pentecost.

THE GREAT MISSIONARY

The Apostle Paul

Saint Paul was born about ten or fifteen years after Christ. He came from a prominent family of an important town, Tarsus. The city was wealthy, very cultured, and a thousand years old. It boasted a population of half a million at the time of Paul. So, Paul was a city boy. That is why his writings do not have the homey comparisons of the Gospels. His epistles are filled with references to games in the stadium, business in the forum, and the great processions that were like our ticker-tape parades.

HIS CONVERSION

Paul inherited Roman citizenship, a powerful status symbol, from his father. Yet he was prouder of being a strict Pharisee. As a Pharisee he belonged to the spiritual and intellectual upper class. Because a good Pharisee was not supposed to take money for teaching the law of God, Paul became a skilled tentmaker.

He stormed onto the biblical stage as a persecutor of Christians. He was on the road to Damascus when he experienced a conversion that changed him completely. Struck to the ground by a light from heaven and touched by God, the angry Pharisee overnight became a militant Christian. After his experience on the Damascus road, Paul retired to the Arabian desert for three years of study and prayer. He needed time to overcome the shock of this event and to understand the meaning of it and of his conversion.

HIS CAREER AS AN APOSTLE BEGINS

When three years were up, Paul returned to Damascus only to find that the Jews now considered him a traitor and were planning to kill him. Like a biblical secret-agent, Paul made the first of many dramatic escapes, this time over the wall in a basket. He went back to his hometown, Tarsus, and worked there for ten years. He was roughly thirty-eight years old.

The New Testament gives some details about Paul's appearance. He was small but sturdy. He had a hooked nose, and eyebrows that met. He was described as both a man and an angel. His critics at Corinth claimed that his bodily presence was weak and his speech very poor.

The real beginning of Paul's career as an apostle occurred at Antioch when Barnabas launched him into the public eye. From there, the two of them sailed on the first of the missionary journeys described in the Acts of the Apostles (13:4–14:25). They sailed from Antioch, landing at some towns on the island of Cyprus.

PAUL'S PROBLEM: THE JEWISH QUESTION

One of the most important problems of Paul's career was the Jewish question. On the surface, the first Christians seemed to be just another Jewish sect. In Jerusalem, they still worshiped in the temple, studied the Old Testament, and kept the diet laws. This is easy to understand, since most of the first Christians were Jews. The Gentiles came later. But the Christian community in Jerusalem established the idea that a Gentile must first become

THE APOSTLE PAUL, *the greatest missionary and the most exciting Christian personality the Church has produced*

a Jew before he could become a Christian. So the Gentile had to be circumcised and observe the dietary laws.

Paul reminded the Jewish Christians that Christ had fought against the tyranny of the Old Testament law. Paul denounced the legalism of the Pharisees. He showed the Jewish Christians that faith and baptism were the real ways to enter the Church. The growing number of Gentile converts made by Paul and Barnabas created a significant opposition to the Jewish Christians' views. The conservative Jerusalem community was shocked that Paul's Gentile communities were not circumcised and ate anything they liked.

Paul's teaching eventually won out. He challenged Peter at Antioch (Galatians 2:11). Then he won approval for his point of view at the Council of Jerusalem (Acts 15). Finally, he was able to teach clearly that all distinctions between Jew and Gentile, Greek and barbarian, had been torn down. The dividing walls that separated men had been demolished by the peace of Jesus Christ (Ephesians 2).

PAUL'S MISSIONARY METHOD

Paul developed a missionary technique that is still in use today. His first job was to organize a community. He moved on when he felt the community could stand on its own feet. He kept in touch with the community through letters and messengers. He always brought the gospel first to the synagogues. Then he would turn to the Gentiles. After a time, the inevitable blowup would come. He had to trust that he would survive riots, stoning, prison, and exile.

He was an administrator as well as an evangelist. Every problem was a new one for him. In Corinth, alone, he had to find a Christian solution for interfaith relations, the end-of-the-world scare, sex problems, dietary laws, women's fashions, and whether Christians should take other Christians to pagan courts. Many of his decisions have influenced Christian policy for centuries.

PAUL THE GREAT MISSIONARY, *often beaten and imprisoned for his dedication to Christ's gospel, finally suffered martyrdom for the faith*

IMPRISONMENT AND MARTYRDOM

Paul's ideas on slavery were not revolutionary, although he did not necessarily support slavery. Many have noted that his heart was in heaven though his feet were always on the earth. In his first letter to the Corinthians, he gave a lofty talk on the gifts of the Spirit, only to end it with: "Now concerning the contribution" (1 Corinthians 16:1). It was precisely "the contribution" which occasioned Paul's ultimate imprisonment and martyrdom. He wanted to go to Rome. First, he had to bring a collection to Jerusalem and, there, defend the Gentile position against the Christians who insisted on keeping circumcision and diet laws. Some Ephesian pilgrims spotted him in the temple and caused an uproar. Paul was almost killed, but was rescued by the police.

An escort of two hundred infantrymen, two hundred spearmen, and seventy cavalrymen took him to Caesarea, where he was imprisoned for two years. Finally, he appealed to Caesar and was taken to Rome after being shipwrecked at Malta.

> And so we came to Rome. And the brethren there, when they heard of us, came as far as the forum of Appius and Three Taverns to meet us. On seeing them Paul thanked God and took courage. . . . And he lived there two whole years at his own expense, and welcomed all who came to him, preaching the kingdom of God and teaching about the Lord Jesus Christ quite openly and unhindered [Acts 28:14–15; 30–31].

Paul was martyred for the faith, probably after the burning of Rome in A.D. 64 during the reign of Nero. He was the greatest missionary and probably the most exciting Christian personality the Church has produced. In the life of Paul, we can find the first fruits of the hope of Jesus.

Index